THE HISTORY OF DEMOCRACY HAS YET TO BE WRITTEN

THE HISTORY OF DEMOCRACY HAS YET TO BE WRITTEN

HOW WE HAVE TO LEARN TO GOVERN ALL OVER AGAIN

Belt Publishing

THOMAS GEOGHEGAN

Printed in the United States of America
First edition 2021
1 2 3 4 5 6 7 8 9

ISBN: 978-1-953368-00-3

Belt Publishing
5322 Fleet Avenue
Cleveland, Ohio 44105
www.beltpublishing.com

Cover art by David Wilson
Book design by Meredith Pangrace

For Susan

TABLE OF CONTENTS

INTRODUCTION:

HOW TO REPRESENT THE PEOPLE

When I was about to be clobbered in my run for Congress, a friend said, "Oh well, at least you'll get a book out of it."

What? You think I'm out here right now, stumbling through ice storms, snow spitting in my face, slipping on stairs to grasp at a doorbell . . . just so I can write a *book*? No! I am damned if there will be a book. No, no, no. Even if it were to sell like *Eat, Pray, Love,* I'll never write a book.

Well, obviously, I did. But this book is not about my campaign. It's about what I learned—at first during the campaign, and then later—about how we might end our country's political divide.

After the Trump Era, we have to start over. We have to learn how to represent ourselves all over again and do it better. We have to figure out how to represent everyone our form of government is currently so bad at representing—the working high school grads, whom I had the presumption to think that as a union-side lawyer I would be representing in the House; or the 100 million nonvoters; or the young, who face environmental Armageddon and for whom we should get out of the way.

The way to genuinely represent them, I am certain, is only in part to change our form of government. To be sure, as I argue, we have to get rid of the US Senate if we want to secure our freedom to act. But we also have to change our whole idea of what representation means—of why it is legitimate in this country to have anyone represent anyone else at all. We're Americans. We all ought to be in office.

Oh, at first I didn't want to write a book. No book! But then I thought: What's the harm in telling one little story?

One bitterly cold December night, ten months after I'd lost, I came home late and parked my car out on the street. As I walked home, a woman, wrapped in a muffler, in the dark, came toward me, click, click, click. As she passed, head down, she said in a low voice:

"I voted for you."

Then—around the corner and she was gone.

Wait!

I went back to my condo, burst open the door, and began to pull out the old candidate flyers and questionnaires. God help me: I *had* run for Congress. Here was a photo of me without my glasses. What was I doing without my glasses?

I remembered saying to the photographer, "No one knows me without my glasses."

"No one knows you anyway," he replied.

And now I saw the candidate questionnaires I'd filled out: from women's groups, gay rights groups, civil rights groups, disability rights groups, Polish groups, Latino groups, the Sierra Club and other environmental groups, and labor unions, of course.

Well, I had run for Congress. Here was the evidence. That was the night, or maybe it was the next night, I started throwing all these things away. Otherwise, when I'm ninety and drooling and in decline, my niece Sarah may say, "Uncle

Tom, do you remember you once ran for Congress?"
    I'd wave my hand: no . . . no.
    "Oh, yes you did! Here are the questionnaires!"
    Now, maybe instead she'll find this book.

It was a special election for a US House seat on the North Side of Chicago that had come open in January 2009 because the incumbent US House member, Rahm Emanuel, had just resigned to become Obama's White House chief of staff. It was, in a way, the first true "post-meltdown" election; the collapse of Lehman Brothers, then AIG, and then the near collapse of capitalism had come too fast in the last weeks of the November 2008 election for many people like me to grasp. Indeed, more than ten years later, it is still hard to grasp. As Adam Tooze wrote in *Crashed* (2018), capitalism itself might have disappeared that year.

It was a utopian moment. And as a union-side lawyer, I thought I might have a chance in the House to get an audience for things I had been saying for years. It seems less apocalyptic now, thanks to the pandemic, but it was our first little brush with the end of the world.

Besides, I had nothing better to do. As a Chicago lawyer, I had spent the 1980s and 1990s, during the first big global shock, filing suits to pick up bits and pieces of pension and severance benefits when the old, unionized steel mills on the South Side began to close. Now, in this century, the unions were gone, and when the remaining plants closed, there were not even little bits and pieces of benefits to get. I thought if I went to Congress, I could make the same arguments for my clients I was making in court. I could pour out my heart into the Congressional Record, instead of to a federal judge's twenty-five-year-old clerks.

Of course, I had no chance.

Except—and this keeps me up at night—I *could* have actually won. The winner, Mike Quigley, got no more than 12,000 votes. That was in the Democratic primary, which in Chicago is, in effect, the main election, as no Republican candidate ever has the faintest chance of winning. He now has a House seat representing 700,000 people, and he did it with just 12,000 votes. That's what haunts me: even if no one knew me, couldn't I get at least 12,000 votes? There are twelve-year-olds on Facebook with 12,000 friends. Yes, it's a judgment on our democracy that you can pick up a House seat with 12,000 votes; the fact that I couldn't is a judgment on me.

When it was over, Violet, the cleaning lady, was the first to say it. She came by just after the election. As she put on her big yellow rubber gloves she said, in her melodious Jamaican voice: "Now *Thomas* . . . you *lost* and now you wasted *all that money.*"

She frowned, looked around. "You could have taken that money and fixed this place up."

She was right—it was all a waste. We raised all of $330,000—I am at a loss as to how—and I came in seventh out of fourteen, right in the middle. A friend said, "Why don't you just say you were in a three-way tie for fourth?" No: I was seventh. Let's use the real words. I let everyone down.

All that money!

I still feel I should be doing some kind of community service to work it off.

I said to my brother, "It could have all gone to feed children in Central America."

"Oh, you can't think of it that way," he said.

"Oh, I think you *can* 'think of it that way,'" I said.

"Then think of it this way," he said. "You took that money and hired all those kids to work for you. You created *jobs*. You were part of the stimulus."

He was right. I *could* think of it that way.

But I don't think of it that way; I still think we should have given it all to feed children in Central America. I knew turnout would be low in a special election, but in this one, just 50,000 people voted to decide who would represent 700,000 people. And this was no ordinary House seat. It was smack dab in Chicago, a red-hot, blazingly blue political city, home of the legendary Machine, a sacred space in the country's political imagination, and still only 50,000 voters could come out.

To get a House seat for 700,000 people with just 12,000 votes—such an election would not be considered legitimate in Belarus or Zaire. But then of late, no election outcome in this country has seemed to be legitimate. And why should anyone accept the outcome of any of our elections as legitimate? In 2016, over 100 million eligible Americans did not even bother to vote.

But all that brooding came later, after Trump came in. Deep down I knew it was a good thing I had lost. If I had won, as a friend said, "It would have been the end of you." He didn't even have to say, "the smiling public man."

I wish now it had been the end of me. Maybe with a big fat public-man smile I might have done a little good. Anyway, for a while it was the end of me. But I am also reminded of something a man once told me about a Texas politician of whom it was said, "He's more like you than you are."

I'd like to set out here how I too, for a few months, was more like you than you are, while also being less like me than ever. Maybe that is what Whitman meant when he wrote of that great word Democracy, "whose history, I suppose, remains unwritten."

But I think he meant it had not even started to happen—and unless and until it does, there is never going to be a book.

CHAPTER ONE:
WHAT I LEARNED
RUNNING FOR CONGRESS

had always had a crush on the House. As a teen, I had treasured the only book to my knowledge that is written just about the US House—*Forge of Democracy* by the reporter Neil MacNeil, published in 1963 and now long out of date. MacNeil made it seem like a serious, even wonky place, where members boned up to become experts on narrow issues, while across the way, senators would fake their way through. But the House is also the battering ram: the People's House, the only part of the Constitution that represents the people as a whole—not by state but by nation, as the American people really are. It's the part that makes the Constitution move.

But until somehow the House gets the upper hand, and is gerrymander-free, there will never be true democracy in the land. We will never have a means to represent the people as a whole.

The framers tried to give it the upper hand. As set out in Article I, every revenue bill has to originate in the House. It was to have the power of the purse. That's why it can shut down the government. It was expected that the House could shut down the government. More than the Bill of Rights, that was a principal way the framers expected to frustrate tyranny.

It also means that the House is the place where we can begin to redistribute income. It is the principal means we have to move to a social democracy.

And while it's the role of the House to be more expert than the Senate, it's also the role of the House to howl. It's the House—as the People's House—that is or should be closer to the working people I represent. It's the House that is supposed to channel the nation's id. It's the House that touches that raw, red, pulsating national wound that so many senators hesitate to touch.

And now I say this with tears: it's the Democrats' failure to hold the House for which I ran in 2009 that wrecked Obama's presidency.

The House is our contribution to civilization, the only place where there is government of, by, and for the people, based on one person, one vote. But the House itself is a wounded institution. The rise of the Senate filibuster—used now in a way unknown in earlier times—has created a huge supermajority that every House bill must pass, and that has kept the House from representing the people or working its will.

And over time, the House became powerless to save itself. All my adult life, I had seen labor law reform bills—under Carter and Clinton and soon under Obama—get through the House and go nowhere in the Senate. Thanks to the filibuster—and the Senate's addiction to supermajority rule—the Senate, by consent of its majority, has used its procedural rules to shut down the House.

For some time, I had been writing op-eds with titles like "The Infernal Senate" and ranting about the filibuster, even years ago, when no one on the left seemed to care. And perhaps I had some idea that if I somehow won a seat in the House, I might do something to save it. But what? What should inspire the US, and those who would try to restore its power, is the

British House of Commons, which, in 1910, persuaded the king to pack the House of Lords with new and more liberal peers to remove it as a check and balance. Of course, the US House cannot appoint new senators, but at least it could howl.

And then one day I realized: *There was an open seat.*

How often does an open seat open up and walk into your life?

It had opened up because Obama had named Rahm Emanuel, representative of the Fifth Congressional District of Illinois, to be the White House chief of staff.

The Fifth District! I had lived in the Fifth District longer than the Fifth itself had, thanks to all the gerrymandering it had gone through. Every ten years its boundaries would bobble around like the borders of a Balkan state, but I had always been smack in its middle. In a prior age, it had been the Machine District, and those who held the seat—like Dan Rostenkowski and Rod Blagojevich, who went on to be governor—were known to be the Machine's special emissaries in Washington, at least until they went to prison. But in 2009, it was held by Emanuel, who had been a dance major at Sarah Lawrence. It was no longer a beer-and-shot-glass district; it was open now to a metrosexual like me.

But that's not why I ran.

That night in November when Obama was elected, I saw the stars fall from the sky. It was as if that twelve-gated city had come down and crashed upon my head. It seemed that night the graves should open and the dead would come out to walk.

It did not occur to me that night to run for the House—I was not even aware that there was now an open seat. I had been out with friends, and, motivated as much by my despair at having done so little to bring about such an astral event, I skipped his speech in Grant Park and went home, vowing to do what I could do to help him, or help anyone. I was sixty years old. To hold back all my life and now go into politics for the first time seemed like waiting until age sixty to start courting the opposite sex. I had no busines doing it. But I lay in bed that night—and this happens every time the Democrats win a presidential election—and thought that he himself was a utopian moment, in his own person. Even now I believe, out of sight, the stars are still falling from the sky.

In Max Weber's phrase, I wanted to put my hand on the wheel of history, or at least a baby finger. I know: a lot of inflated self-importance. Normally nothing would have come of it. But then that seat in my own district opened up and no one important was claiming it.

And I wanted to help prove the country was governable.

I never actually decided to run. Or, I never made a final decision. Oh yes, I was egging myself on. No one else did. I had to bring it up with friends in a certain way so I did not seem vain or could later disclaim any idea of running. Here's a line I would try out:

"Say, you know, I look at these people running . . ."

"Yeah, no one special, really . . ."

"Yeah, really, I was thinking I might as well go for it . . ."

And I'd wait to see if he or she laughed. Count one, two, three, four. If they laughed, I would laugh.

"Yeah, sure—why *don't* you go for it?"

That's how your friends can talk you into running.

Here's what the pros say: "*Never* listen to your friends— they will always tell you to run." It excites them, right?

"Go for it. We need you in office."

Or: "Do it, at least I'll have someone to vote for."

No, no, the pros say, don't listen to your friends! Look—do you even know the boundaries of the district? Do you know, for example, where North Lake Central is? And you'll need at least a million dollars: how are you going to get that?

It's true I never made a final decision to run—I just found myself doing it. But I do remember, over Thanksgiving, in Cincinnati, jogging with my brother (a different brother, not the one in the introduction, as I have five of them).

Between breaths, I was saying to him. "I've not told you . . . but I'm . . . I'm thinking of running for Congress."

"What . . . like what's holding . . . you . . . back?"

"Yeah, I really want to write . . . a book, on labor, in Germany . . . and . . . I should probably finish . . . it . . ."

"Wait, you'd . . . give up a shot at . . . *Congress* . . . just to write a book?"

So I went back to Chicago—where there were now more candidates for the seat—and I called up Rita. She had been working on campaigns since 1972, when, as a mere child, she had helped pull off the unseating of the Daley delegates at the Democratic convention.

"Rita, I have no idea what to do."

"You have to set up an exploratory committee. You just can't start running. It looks vain."

It seemed vainer to do that—but I didn't know.

"And when you announce," she said, "the press will want to know how much you have in pledges."

"No, this isn't going to work."

"Look, here's what you need to do. This weekend, come up with a list of fifty people who'll support you."

Fifty!

By Sunday I was only up to twenty; it was hard. But I kept

going. I got to thirty. I almost gave up. Come on, I thought, get to forty. And late Sunday night I had fifty. The next day I gave the list to Rita.

"This is a good list," she said. "Now you need fifty more."

"Fifty more? I thought I was done!"

She laughed. "No, no, you're just getting started."

It was now early December, when I always lose heart. Every day it was darker. I wanted to go to sleep, not run for Congress. More friends now told me to run. "Hey, at least I'll have someone to vote for!" Even Kitty; she was a political consultant. "You have absolutely no chance," she said. "But you should do it anyway. People like you—once they do it, they'll never do it again, but they'll never regret it."

Still undecided, I began to interview for a campaign manager. I had no idea who was qualified or who I really wanted. Then I met Julie. She said, "I will make one promise to you. I can't promise you will win, but I can promise you this—when the campaign is over, *you will not be in debt.*"

I gave her the job.

Just after she was hired, she set a test for me. It came the night of my birthday, and Julie and my brother and his wife and a few others went out to the Brauhaus, which had a dance floor and two musicians, both Latino, perhaps Puerto Rican, in little Alpine pants and beanies.

I opened a present—long underwear, from Dan and Mary. "You'll need it."

Julie looked at me hard and said, "I want you right now to go over to the band members and tell them you're running for Congress and want their vote."

"You mean . . . now?"

"I want to see you go over and say, 'Hi, I'm Tom

Geoghegan, I'm a Democrat, I'm running for Congress, and I need your vote.'"

"I . . . I can't . . . He's busy playing the accordion."

"Go."

I started toward the band. I froze. I looked back at Julie. *Go on.*

I got up to the two guys and shut my eyes and said, "I'm Tom . . . Geoghegan, and I'm-sorry-to-bother-you-but-I'm-running-for-Congress-and-would-like-your . . ."

I turned to Julie: Is that enough?

No, the bartender, too. Oh hell, OK—I did the bartender.

When I sat down and Julie smiled, I knew it was for real. I was a candidate. Two weeks later, no one could stop me from shaking hands.

It is hard to distinguish now one day from the other. It was hard even then. But in just a few weeks, here is what I had learned.

Lesson One: Account for Every Second

I had started later than the other thirteen candidates, and I had been mistaken about the time until the primary. Under the law, the governor was empowered to schedule the primary election (the only election that counted in Chicago) ninety days from the time the vacancy in the House arose. Everyone told me: "The governor never sets it any sooner." Only this time he did. On January 4, 2009, when he issued the writ of election, they cut the time to sixty days. I really had no chance now. I had to raise money, then get out the flyers, then—no, it was impossible. I was in too deep to get out—or to have a moment of lucidity.

Two politician friends, Deborah and Larry, took me to a bar and tried to console me. I was in despair. I was already too late to get the trial lawyers, who were already committed to other candidates. Deborah said, "Look, the others will have more money, and they are going to have more endorsements, but there is one way in which you are going to be the equal to the others. There are just twenty-four hours in a day. For every candidate, there is the same number of hours in the day. In that way, you're all starting equal from here."

In *The Cloud of Unknowing*, written in the fourteenth century, the anonymous author, a mystic, says each of us will be held accountable for every instant. He could be writing to a political candidate.

I remember Julie once told me she saw no need for a staffer to stay overnight in my apartment. She said, "We thought you were entitled to *that* much privacy."

Wait—that was even considered?

Of course, they had to keep their eye on me. For example, in the afternoon, I like to walk to a Starbucks to get coffee. "Oh no, you stay here. We'll get it for you."

"Please, let me go. Don't you *see*. I want the walk *to* the Starbucks more than I want the Starbucks!"

It was like having a girlfriend again. "Those cufflinks, let's button those." "You're set for a haircut." "I think you need some shirts." "We bought you a few handkerchiefs."

"Here's a breath mint." Really—do you think I need it?

And if I had to account for every instant, it was due to my weeks of dithering: should I run, should I not? I understood better the line in *Richard II*: "I wasted time, and now doth time waste me."

I had told a friend I could work in the law office in the morning, then campaign in the afternoon. I mean, I had to keep the practice going.

"You think you're going to do this *part-time*?"

"Well, can't you? I mean—members of Congress, they don't spend *all* their time campaigning."

They don't—do they?

So I had to be watched. In a few weeks, Julie had hired a young Northwestern grad to be my "body man" and drive me around. Because kids like him from the suburbs screw up parallel parking, I often had to take the wheel. But he had great political gifts. I should have been the body man and driver, and he should have run.

Every morning at 5:30 a.m., I would lie wide-awake, waiting for my front bell to ring, waiting for the body man to collect my body—that is, for J. to take me to the El (the rapid transit line) to start shaking hands.

Such a decent young man, but as I lay there waiting for him to buzz from downstairs at 5:30 a.m., I hated him with all my heart, as he must have hated me. He had already been up since 5:00 and gone out in a shrieking wind, with twenty-below windchill, to stand until it was 5:30 so he could ring the bell. I was only the second most miserable person in Chicago.

Here is my advice to a new candidate. Make sure you knit up the raveled sleeve of care *in advance*. Macbeth would have murdered sleep, or at least his own, just by going into politics.

I read that Senator Chuck Grassley was at the Senate gym every morning at 4:00 a.m. I started having nightmares that I might win the election. Then I'd wake and lie there, waiting for J. and the buzzer to buzz.

Lesson Two: It's All about the Weather
That's what my brother who coached Little League told me, but it's true of politics as well. I already knew that politics

was a blood sport, but the shock was to find it is also played outdoors.

The Chicago Machine insisted on holding the primary in the dead of a Leningrad-type winter to stop independents like me. It was to crush democracy movements without turning on a fire hose. Now the Machine was dead, or on life support, and to keep holding the primary in winter was not just cruel but pointless.

I used to tell people, "If I had known it would be so cold, I never would have run." They think I am joking.

I had come to believe winter was no big deal, but I now realized I had spent those winters indoors with just fleeting little waits for the El. Now I was at the same El stops for an hour, two hours, three, and stamping my feet, I could feel my toes go numb, then my feet, as if instead of feet, I had legs on two blocks of ice. If I tried to walk, someone had to hold me. At least when I went door-to-door, I could keep moving. Now I could knock on doors only on the weekend. On a weekday, no one was at home. Being responsible people, most of the "repeat" voters who would vote in a special election had day jobs in the Loop. And even on Saturday or Sunday, it was dark by 4:00 p.m. or earlier, so unlike summer, when I could have campaigned for hours until sunset at 8:00 p.m. or later, I had what seemed like minutes just on these two dark winter weekend days. Later, I found out from a spreadsheet done by Tom Leuthner, a friend and gifted number cruncher, that by far, the majority of my votes came from a few precincts in the Forty-Seventh Ward, where I did not live and where I knew no one, but where I had knocked on doors. If I had started earlier or had another month, or been able to go until 8:00 p.m., I could have at least tripled the number of votes.

In fact, it was so cold that even on a sunny Saturday, if I started at 10:00 a.m., I would be done by noon—and maybe, if I could defrost myself, I could try again from 2:00 to 3:00. I also had to make sure I had someone go with me, like my brother Dan or Tony, and we wore buttons and had literature so we would *look* like candidates and so people would at least consider opening the door. But even if I had someone with me, to make it look official, I still had to give up before the sun set at 4:00 p.m.

Yes, I wanted to keep going—I wasn't even tired—but as I would say to Dan or Tony or J., "There's an hour of light, I know . . . and I'm not tired . . . but I can't talk . . ."

My face would freeze.

One of my lines was, "I want to raise Social Security." But after two hours going door-to-door, I could not make the "S" sound. You try it. Stand thirty minutes in five-below windchill, then try to say, "Social Security."

Not only did I freeze, but back in the campaign office, still in my long underwear, I would come close to boiling to death.

Yes, men and women did open the doors to hear my pitch. They seemed astonished to see anyone out there in the snow. "Wait, you're the candidate? I can't believe it. Wait here—I want to get my wife. Mary! This guy, he's a candidate for Congress!"

These were repeat voters. Because turnout would be so small in a special election, we targeted those who showed up, no matter what, at every kind of election. Yet, because the primaries were in ten-below windchill, I doubt that except for a few of them, they had not seen a candidate in years.

True, the older voters might recall precinct captains, and in the west side of the Fifth District some still exist. One woman over there told me, "Yes, I have to put a sign in the yard for one of the people running against you—but don't worry, I'm voting for you."

Yet worse than the windchill was the rock salt—or I should say, the windchill *and* the rock salt. The best place to reach both sides of the district was to stand at the Blue Line El stop at Lawrence Avenue, midway between the gentrified east and working-class west, or at least it still seemed the midpoint at that time. The Blue Line runs from O'Hare to the Loop and alongside the Kennedy Expressway right in the median strip, four lanes of diesel trucks on one side and four lanes of diesel trucks on the other. Even now, years later, when I drive past the Lawrence El stop, for just a few seconds I have a kind of PTSD, like a solider after a war. The Kennedy divides the Fifth, divides the city, divides the United States of America. It is a gaseous Mississippi, roaring and poisonous, and above the din of it all, I could taste the rock salt as I screamed:

"Tom Geoghegan!"

"Democrat!"

"Running for Congress!"

Even as I write, I can taste the rock salt that the diesel trucks were spitting up.

Lesson Three: When Fourteen Are in the Race, You Can Say Whatever You Want

There were candidate forums that all fourteen of the candidates running—and then just twelve of us, after two dropped out—used to attend. Each of us had sixty seconds to answer a question like, "The economy is collapsing. What would you do to save it?" By the time I got going, a little girl would pop up, waving a card: fifteen seconds!

I'd stop, then start, and she was right back up: five seconds!

Then right back up, hopping up and down: time's UP!!

All right, little girl, I see you.

I would sit down in despair. Mike Quigley, the front-runner, never took up a whole minute. He had one answer for everything: "I'm for transparency."

I too should have said I was for transparency and left it there. But I wanted to say where I stood on some issues. I had three, on the rule that people could only remember three:

Raise Social Security—Not just save it, but raise it, from 39 percent or so on average of working income to 50 percent.

Single-Payer Healthcare—Because otherwise, with employer-based health insurance, and the waste of the whole system, no working person will ever get a wage increase. Besides, if we lower the nonwage costs that employers now pay, we might shift more production into goods and not services. I believe single-payer healthcare would reduce a trade deficit that depletes us of more manufacturing jobs every year.

And finally:

Stop the Bailout—That is, Obama's proposed bailout of the big banks. In part I said it because everyone else on the left was saying it. I always made sure to add that I was all for the bailout if in turn we had public trustees serve as watchdog directors on all these banks that were too big to fail.

I began to hear myself in dreams:

Raise Social Security.

Single-payer healthcare.

Stop the bailout.

I spit it out at the El. I said it as I slipped down doorsteps. I screamed it on the Kennedy. Without mentioning labor, which might gross out some voters, I was running as a labor lawyer. I was trying to appeal to the alienated white working class: "Be reconciled to us Democrats!" As a labor lawyer, I have a sense of the worst thing that happened—something too many people fail to see. It was not the reduction in wages, though that did happen in real terms, but the disappearance of the old, defined-benefit private pension plans. Keynes told us that a reduction of money wages would set off a revolt, and in the loss of these plans, it happened invisibly. We still live with the consequences—Trump was just one of them—and we're not done yet.

If I had had a campaign slogan—and I didn't—it would have been "We have to get all of us out of debt." Personal debt, student debt, consumer debt, trade deficit debt, and even government debt. Yes, I know: Keynes is in favor of it. So is Paul Krugman, in just about every column he writes. So am I! But it's a bad thing. It transfers money from the debtor class to the creditor class. No, we have to get wages up instead.

Of course, the pros were right: Keep it simple. But I didn't want to keep it simple. It may be dumb to run on the issues, but no one will bother you if you do. But I couldn't afford TV spots, and in the printed press, there wasn't a news hole left to fit in any of us who were running. Both the local papers, the *Tribune* and the *Sun-Times*, seemed to disappear in 2009, at least temporarily. The former shock jock briefly in charge of the *Tribune* had cut it to pieces. And the *Sun-Times* had already shrunk to the size of a "shopper" at KMart.

But one local paper was still going: the *New York Times*. On the day I announced, I managed to get an op-ed in the paper of record on the issue I cared most about—the way the Senate afflicted our democracy. Governor Blagojevich had just been caught trying to sell Obama's Senate seat. He had the power under state law to forego a special election and appoint an unelected senator for the remainder of Obama's term. "I've got this thing, and it's fucking golden," he said, fool enough not to know he was being taped. But it was my chance to hit at the Senate and hammer home how perhaps 20 percent of senators since the ratification of the Seventeenth Amendment had gotten in by these appointments, without being elected by the people at all.

It is only the House that is the People's House.

I had hoped this bribe for a Senate seat might be a campaign issue, but we were used to Illinois governors going to prison. In Mid-campaign, our little firm sued the governor to have a special election to fill the Obama vacancy. Julie had put up with my doing it, but the only time she became angry with me—and was right to be—was when I also started working on a brief. I wanted the House to be the People's House more than I wanted to be one of the people in it.

Lesson Four: Learn to Do Your Own Dirty Work
Here are the three worst things I did as a candidate:

I bought signatures to get on the ballot. Look, it was too cold to stand in front of Walgreens with a clipboard, in five-below windchill. So I outsourced it to a vendor.

I did a robocall. I am sorry if you got one. I only did it once.

I did cold calls to total strangers.

Every weekday, from 10:00 a.m. to noon, with a staffer standing over me, I did cold calls for money. No one in our firm believed I could make these calls. Our office manager said, "You can't even ask people who owe you to pay you money, so how are you going to ask people who don't owe you money at all?

It's easy: just stop thinking of them as people.

I went to Peter, who had done this kind of thing, for counseling.

"Peter, look at this name, I can't call him. He's a labor lawyer like me, and a friend, he's got two children in college, and look, what's the 'ask'? It's $500! I can't just—"

Peter said, "Call 'im!"

"Like that—I mean, how do I . . .?"

"Call 'im!"

"Look, how do I call up—this guy, he's the former Cook County assessor . . . I can't just call up the former—"

"Call 'im!"

And that's what I had to keep playing in the right side of the brain: "Call 'im!" Don't think. "Call 'im!"

Another time I took a friend, Chris, to lunch. I knew he had money. I just couldn't do the ask. I broke down. I just started fumbling: "Chris, I just hate to ask . . . you know, I just can't ask . . . I can't . . ."

He stopped me. He was curt. "You should learn to ask for money. It's a good skill to acquire."

I was stung by this. "OK," I said, "will you give me $250?"

There was a pause. "I have to think about it."

Ah!

Once, I just flat-out stopped: "I can't do this anymore." The staff looked aghast. If I stopped, they wouldn't eat. Todd, the senior adviser, said, "Come on, let's go for a walk." Out in the hall, I said, "These are my friends I'm calling—I can't do this."

He said, "Do you understand? No one is going to give you money they don't have."

"No?"

"No."

"I guess not." It occurred to me I was vain to think they would. Whether I asked my friends, or didn't ask them, it's all vanity, really.

"For the people who give," Todd said, "it's like gambling."

"You're right." I get it. I was just like a horse—or something. I started to calm down. I went back in to pick up the phone. And though I made far more money because friends like Rick and Kathy and others sent out emails to *their* friends, at least I can say: I did go on.

And to go on builds character, as it must have done for Barack Obama. When he first ran for the Senate, a friend asked me if I wanted to go to a fundraiser for him. It was at the home of David Axelrod, who said, "I've never held a fundraiser for my own client. But Barack Obama is special." And then Obama talked and it was true; he was like Lincoln. It seemed hopeless for him, though. No one was there, really. I looked around the room: it was just Ned and me and a few others, and Ned and I had no money. I felt sorry for him. He wasn't going anywhere.

Axelrod did not make the pitch at the end. Obama, the candidate, did, and did it with a kind of pride. "I know someone else is supposed to make the pitch," he said. "*But I like to do my own dirty work.*"

It was so French, and cool, and existential. It had to follow that he was a smoker.

And while I said I did only three shameful things, I admit doing one more thing that embarrassed me.

I went to Hollywood for money.

It was my brother's brother-in-law who made it happen.

He had worked as a political consultant on one of Jerry Brown's campaigns. I had had no sleep and can remember nothing except that I can see myself standing next to a man who might have been Tom Hayden.

I had never been to Hollywood, or California, and what surprised me in the thirty-six sleepless hours I spent there was how serious and well-informed everyone was.

But maybe this wasn't Hollywood—maybe I am getting this mixed-up with some other place.

Lesson Five: I Have No Clout with Organized Labor, or with Working-Class Voters Either

My law partner, Leon Despres, who had just turned 100 years old—and was now rarely in the office—called it: maybe 50,000 people would vote, and I had no chance unless I had a big local endorse me. I needed SEIU or AFSCME or the Chicago Teachers Union to put in $150,000 and turn out the vote. I went to the Chicago Federation of Labor and begged: "I have been a union-side lawyer, a labor lawyer, fighting for you guys ever since law school. If I get in the House, I will be working twenty-four hours a day to bring back a real labor movement."

I held my breath. Everything turned on this meeting. Julie, sitting next to me, knew it too.

The CFL president nodded. "I'd like to help. I heard from a lot of people in Washington . . ." He meant the AFL-CIO. "I guess you've got a lot of friends there. The problem is, in Chicago, a lot of our people don't know you."

He was right. It was only later that we did a few cases for the Chicago Teachers Union, after Karen Lewis took over as president. The unions we represented at this time—like the local conferences of the Brotherhood of Locomotive Engineers and Trainmen—were out of town.

"Yes," I said, "but I'm the labor lawyer in this race."

"We're not really worried who wins. Whoever wins, they're going to listen to us."

So then I tried a few locals where I at least knew the presidents. "Well," one said, "we like you, but we're going to go with Fritchey." John Fritchey was a state legislator. "He did us a favor once."

"OK, he did you a favor once—but I have poured out my whole life, fighting for labor."

Another local president—whom I love—did take pity. He took me out to lunch. "Look," he said, "we did a poll, and no one has ever heard of you."

Then he said what was true but what I hated to hear. "If you really want to go into politics, why don't you think of becoming an alderman?"

I had to keep from saying: "I'd rather die." I didn't want to go into politics—I wanted to be in the House or to at least prove I could get in by appealing to working-class voters whom the Democrats had lost.

I wanted to prove that it was possible to end the divide on the kinds of issues I was raising. It was a fantasy. I would win the election, and then having proved the point, I would resign. I didn't want to be in the House gym on a bike at 4:00 a.m.

I did get a few labor endorsements—both of the nurse unions, the IBT Local 743, taxi drivers, and a few rank-and-file groups. And I had plenty of volunteers from the staffs of the big-name locals in the city. And I told myself, "It might be better not to have a big local endorse me and give me $250,000. Then it would own me. Even if I believed heart and soul in everything the local did—even if it were the noblest cause on the planet—even if they were purer and humbler than the mendicant Little Sisters of the Poor, I would know deep down that somebody owned me."

Meanwhile, I found out that as a candidate—out of my role as a labor lawyer—I was afraid of the working class too. I was used to going into bars and giving updates on lawsuits while guys drank and watched the Bears game. I had their attention: I was there to talk about their money. Now, as a candidate, if I went into an American Legion Post, no one bothered to look up. I had lost my karma. It seemed dangerous to approach people at the bar. Who the fuck are you? I stood there, and then from all the cigarette smoke, I started coughing and decided to leave.

As mentioned before, the Kennedy Expressway—I-90/I-94—cut the Fifth Ward in two. To the east of the Kennedy, it was yoga classes and Trader Joe's and wine bars that charged eight dollars a glass. To the west, it was Dunkin' Donuts as far as one could see, and in the parishes, people walked up to communion in T-shirts that said "Mama Bear" and "Pokémon." All of us candidates were from the east side, though one or two had a *pied-à-terre* or law office in the west.

There were few Black people in the Fifth because of the intense segregation of the city—though at least in the west, there were now plenty of Muslims, Filipinos, and Latinos, as well as many Polish-speaking Poles. But it was all beyond my reach. It was like trying to rouse a conquered province. People had little time or interest in the People's House, and I went into every twenty-four-hour grill I could and I felt just as powerless over these working-class people as the labor movement is.

Oh sure, I can say that I didn't have enough time, that I didn't have enough money. That the election came up too fast. But on election day west of the Kennedy, there were precincts where no one voted.

Lesson Six: Everyone Has a Vote

Early on, Todd, who did a lot of elections, said, "Be ready—you will find as a candidate that people look at you in a way they never did before." Maybe—and I looked at them as I never had before. A friend who is a Jesuit said that part of his daily prayer was just to sit on the El and look at the faces of those whom no one noticed and who did not expect to be noticed. It would light every El car with a holy fire: every rider seemed transfigured. For me, each rider was transfigured too. *Everyone had a vote: the same, identical, no more and no less than I did.* It gave each of them a certain power over me, and at the same time, I had a certain power over them. As a candidate, in a tie and a suit and a button, and with someone with a clipboard standing next to me, I could go up to anyone and say, "Tom Geoghegan, Democrat, running for Congress." I used to come down hard on the "t" in Democrat to make it sound dangerous, as if to say, "I am with the party." I touched people: with gloves on, yes, because it was cold. But I reached out and took the person's hand. As a bachelor, and long out of any relationship, I had not touched anyone in years. No one shrank from taking my hand, nor did I shrink from taking a hand that was often colder than the dead hand of the Duchess of Malfi, and I would be touched in a different sense when they said:

"Good luck."

Or: "Good luck!"

Or: "Good luck!!"

Many said it without knowing who I was or without even being able to hear over the roar of the Metra train.

As Tony said, "It restores your faith in human nature."

In a mosque, I chatted up taxi drivers after the Friday sermon, and before I did my three issues, I would say: "Salaam alaikum." Later, at 4:00 p.m., I went to the fish fry at St. Pascal's and talked to the early diners, couples who were in their eighties and often deaf. J. came to pull me away. "We have to go." "No, wait, there are two more tables I haven't hit." "We can't—Julie says we have to go."

Ah!

I hated leaving a fish fry just as much as I hated to leave the mosque. I wish now I could have gone into more nursing homes, but I was told to wait to the last minute, no more than two or three days before the election; otherwise, they forget your name. I even went into a tattoo parlor and tried to shake the hands of two kids who were being tattooed.

Each taxi driver, old lady, and tattooed kid had the same equal vote: these are the people for whom we have the People's House. I know the power that a Koch brother or a Sheldon Adelson has, but it is easy to forget that like every person on that El car, they only get one vote. Every person I passed was the bearer of a special cargo which I hoped he or she would give up to me.

After the election, I went through withdrawal. I now had to check myself: "I can't just go up to this person." It was sad. It took two months to go back to noticing people I passed.

There is now an elderly barista whom I see every day at a Starbucks, and I have yet to ask her name.

Lesson Seven: It's Easy to Lose Control over Your Story

One day, I heard our volunteers on the phone reading from a script: "I'm calling for . . . and after he got out of Harvard Law School, he turned down jobs at big corporate law firms to blah, blah, blah . . ."

Aghast, I went to Julie. "I didn't 'turn down jobs at big corporate firms.' I went to work for a union."

Also, I didn't like leading with "Harvard Law School." Not only do I try to keep that to myself, but I also try to keep it *from* myself.

It seemed I had stopped it. But a few days later, in the campaign office, I heard our volunteers saying the same thing. Even worse, one day I picked up one of the new brochures and was shocked to read, "And every Sunday you can find him at the 6:30 evening Mass at St. Benedict's." I felt ill: do we have to put this in a four-color glossy brochure?

Besides, I was worried it might embroil me in *Roe v. Wade*, and I would be denounced by the cardinal, even if I said I personally oppose abortion. But what bothered me more was that I had violated my own privacy. I mean—I'm all for saying I was Catholic, even making a big deal of it.

I just didn't want to put it in a brochure to hand out on the street.

Lesson Eight: I Am Not a Good Enough Person

On Election Day, I knew I would be clobbered. Julie had done her best, but we were still just getting out our literature. My brother came by to get me out of the office and to drop more brochures, however pointless it seemed to be. And it's true—on election night, we had a party in a bar, and it was heartbreaking. Kitty was right: I had learned my lesson, and

I would never do this again.

A few years ago, I had lunch with a law school classmate whom some predicted would end up in the Senate. But he never went into politics. "Early on," he said, "I was able to see close up how politicians live, how you have to be available to people day and night—and I just realized, I'm not capable of doing it; I'm not a good enough person."

I didn't want to do it either. On election night, I felt bad for the staff, for the volunteers—but I have to admit, I also felt relieved it was over and that I was never going to do this again. I stood in the bar and thanked everyone, and for an instant, it crossed my mind to say:

"I know at the beginning, some of you doubted I could put myself out there. 'Oh, he's so reclusive, and he just reads a lot of books.' Well, as you all know, I proved I could put myself out there. I extended myself to other people—more than many might have believed. And so tonight, having done all of that, I just have one more thing to say to everybody: *from now on, everyone, just leave me alone.*"

Well, that might not have struck the right note.

Later that night, Todd asked me what the most surprising thing had been that I had learned as a candidate.

What surprised me was—I had so much time to think. It was a by-product of being "the Product." The staff took care of everything. It gave me a taste of what it might be like to go into assisted living.

I had time to think about the House being the battering ram, and changing the Constitution, and even in what sense the history of democracy is still yet to be written. But I did not think the Trump Era was about to come.

As it turned out, I had another way of getting to

Washington. And it was a good thing I did, because the House of my dreams would become the House of our nightmares after 2010.

CHAPTER TWO:

CHANGE THE COURTS

A few days after I lost the election, I went back into the government as an ordinary lawyer in our system of federal courts, which do the real day-to-day governing of the country. A few months later, I even had a stop on Olympus: in September of 2009, I won a case, nine to zero, in the US Supreme Court.

Yes, I can say I still ended up going to Washington. But as a private-sector lawyer, I can be just as much in the federal government out here in Chicago, or in Boston, or in any of the other places that federal judges are sitting. All these lower federal courts collectively have far more power than the US Supreme Court or federal agencies—and if I could choose, I'd rather appoint all the district and appellate court judges in this country than those justices known as the Nine.

The US Supreme Court distracts us from this real deep state; it even distracts many sensible pundits. It distracts us from the real way we are being governed. Watching the US Supreme Court as we do is like watching episodes of *The Crown,* inasmuch as it helps anyone understand the real way the country is governed. It is a mistake just to focus on the court, or who is on it, just as it is a mistake to think that Washington, DC, exists only or even mostly within DC. The real Washington, DC, is just as much out here, in St. Louis or Phoenix or Miami, where the federal judges sit, as the real Roman Empire was in the provincial cities where its proconsuls were. Except under our form of government, these proconsuls serve for life, and we are not nearly as good as the Antonine emperors in keeping track of them. There may be quality control, of a kind, at the time of confirmation, but then that quality control stops for the next thirty or forty years. There is no Cicero to try them back in the Senate for malfeasance, no Edmund Burke to indict a Warren Hastings. There is not much real governing in Washington, DC, a fact that once led Paul Krugman to describe the federal government as an insurance company operating Social Security and Medicare with a sideline in defense. But Krugman's seeing only the most visible part, not the dark matter made up of all these black-robed judges. The federal courts do the governing of the world: intellectual property, labor, speech, police, race, corporate deals, everything, everything, and everything. Every day, at a morning status call, the entire world rolls into the courtroom. Yes, the federal courts, unlike the state courts, are courts of limited jurisdiction—limited in the sense that the universe itself is limited. Once asked by his son how he determines jurisdiction, a federal judge said, "If I like the case, I have jurisdiction." So while the judiciary may look like the weakest branch, and purports to defer to Congress, the entire lower bench as a body is much more capable at governing than the US House, which, thanks to the Senate, is often incapable of governing at all. In an antitrust case, a single federal judge can decide, as the US House cannot, how much power a company like Google can exercise over the land.

Yet who has even more power in our republic than all these lower court federal judges?

We lawyers do. Because we lawyers decide what cases they are forced to hear.

During the campaign, I used to wonder: Am I allowed to keep filing lawsuits as a lawyer if I am elected to the US House? It's hard for me to imagine that I would give up so much power just to sit there with 434 members and cast a vote that never decided anything one way or the other. I made a note to myself: "Ask the Speaker if I may keep suing people."

We lawyers have incredible power to pull you in to have your deposition for three hours under oath; we have the power to make you recover from your hard drive all those documents you tried to delete the night before we sued you. If that is not a license to kill, it is at least a license to break and enter. It is the right—in a pretrial period that may last for years—to poke through your house, or your business, and ask what you have in that drawer, or over in that box, and while this poking around goes on for years, the judges who have the case may only check in occasionally to see what is going on.

This does not happen in any democracy that does its governing through a functioning legislative branch.

While off campaigning, I had already missed the filing of a complaint and the performance of all the other rites that stop just short of human sacrifice. I had missed this form of public reasoning—"the law"—a kind of reasoning that has nothing to do with substantive rationality, which is something you might engage in at a bar after work.

And it is surrounded with ritual: like baseball and Sunday Mass. It is hard to overstate the number of "good mornings" that are said during a federal judge's status call on any weekday—these are the occasions, at least in Chicago, when perhaps up to a hundred lawyers may be in different courtrooms to attend a status call.

Good morning, Your Honor, [NAME HERE] for the plaintiff.

Good morning, [NAME HERE].

Good morning, Your Honor, [OTHER LAWYER'S NAME] for defendant.

Good morning, [NAME HERE].

Good morning, Your Honor . . .

And so on.

There may be six or seven such *good mornings* from counsel who come up when a case is called and *good mornings* back from the judge.

Like in the Beatles song on *Sgt. Pepper's Lonely Hearts Club Band*, I imagine the pealing of it all over the Loop: GOOD MORNING! GOOD MORNING!

This is the morning in America that counts: the start to every morning of the day-to-day governance of this country. But this governing is not the kind that so many young people applying to law school imagine. From time to time, I get a call from a young person—prompted by a parent-friend—and the question is whether to go to law school.

"Is there some reason you want to be a lawyer?"

"I'm interested in public policy."

"If that's your interest, I wouldn't go to law school. Why not get a degree in public policy?"

"But I thought . . . I thought lawyers . . ."

Do public policy? I find if I'm down to arguing public policy, I've probably lost the case. It's hard to get across: yes, you *are* part of a government, but one that is counting on you not to do public policy. Leave that to someone else. You are supposed to be in a business. You are supposed to make money. Even I, whom some friends think of as a mendicant friar, am obsessed with meeting our payroll, or nut, as Hanna puts it, every month. Your first duty is to the client, not the public interest—and nowhere is that truer than in a public interest case, which may enrage the Right and destabilize the republic.

It's also the adversarial system—some have compared a lawsuit to a surgery with two doctors standing over a patient that one of the doctors is trying to save and the other is trying to kill. Also, the doctors are trying to kill each other. I warn young people who think they will be doing public policy: no, the first thing you have to do is to keep from being killed.

And sure enough, horrified, many young law graduates will bow out—and should. It's the world's most overrated job. But what right do I have to say that? Some years ago, with my law partner, Leon Despres, who died at age 101 and never fully retired, I had dinner with a group that included a young woman who was applying to law school. Leon—or Len—told me later, "When I think of such a lively young woman throwing away three years of her life in a law school down in Champaign-Urbana . . ." He stopped.

Lincoln would have wept.

Yet a lawyer is in the government, and I was glad to be back at it. It does have some of the glamor of government. And yes, while the lower federal courts do most of the real governing, the US Supreme Court does the big decisions.

My friend Anatol Lieven—who is British—said once, "It's just shocking the role that the US Supreme Court plays in your country. In no other country [that is, a mature democracy] do the courts get to make so many decisions." And it is a common complaint: "The court is so political." "Look at what Mitch McConnell did." "Oh my God, look at Amy Coney Barrett." "We have to depoliticize the court." "We have to pack the court."

Here is the answer to Anatol: We need the court because we do not have parliaments or true representative government or majority rule, as the United Kingdom does—or sometimes does, at least. Instead, we have a form of government in which nothing gets decided. Slavery goes undecided until we have a Civil War. Jim Crow went undecided until the Supreme Court issued *Brown v. Board.*

Here may be the better answer to Anatol: If the court seems like an alternative to representative government, it's only because representative government, under our Constitution, is not a viable alternative in the first place.

So can anything be done, other than to pack the court with liberals if we ever get the chance? I think packing the court will make everything worse by politicizing the court even more. The only way to fix the court is to fix Congress instead. *Free the Congress*—as much as possible—from the gridlock that the Constitution imposes on it. Or at least free it from the gridlock that, in the case of the filibuster and other rules, Congress imposes on itself.

If Congress were really the People's House, we would feel less need to pack the court, because the court would be less important. If Congress could free itself to act with dispatch, it could dispose of far more "problems of the penumbra," which so troubled the great British legal theorist H. L. A. Hart, and which we depend so heavily on the court to do. Hart is the advocate of legal formalism, and Hart and his disciples see the role of the court as fitting together formal rules, almost like a puzzle, without worrying about ideals or principles or public interest. Being British, maybe he assumes that there is a single efficient legislative body, like a parliament, based on one person, one vote and capable of turning out the rules that eliminate a lot of the gaps in his scheme of rules. Yes, even in the UK, there may be problems at the penumbra—but if the gap is big enough, Hart's parliamentary body is likely to fix it. The gaps that are left are little bitty ones. In the US, they are bigger than the mountains on Mars, with the two houses of Congress too gridlocked to fix them. It is beyond Congress to do even a little tweak, on which a large majority agree, because it is just beyond the strength of one chamber or another, much less both. Of course, in theory, the court should not legislate— but if it did not, the Constitution would collapse.

Take, for example, *Bostock v. Clayton County,* decided in the 2019–2020 term. By a six to three vote, the court held that Title VII of the Civil Rights Act of 1964 barred job discrimination against LGBT Americans. That was a big "problem of the penumbra." Under a better constitution, with true majority rule, a parliament-like body would have solved "the problem of the penumbra" by one fix or another. But under ours, it is too much to ask. There is too much divided government, too many vetoes, too many senators who, representing as few as 8 percent of the electorate, can stop a law. So it's up to the Supreme Court to figure out how to apply a law passed in *1964.* And H. L. A. Hart may be aghast, and my friend Anatol may find it very disturbing, but if we did not have the court deciding *Bostock* and the lower courts deciding a thousand other things, the country would fall apart. It is mistakenly thought that "checks and balances" refers to the legislative and executive branches, as Montesquieu originally conceived of them. But when the framers used that term, as Garry Wills has pointed out, they were referring to checks and balances between the two chambers of Congress: the whole purpose of the Constitution was to booby-trap the Congress. And that led to what the framers failed to see—that the court, which they did not booby-trap, is left to decide by five to four or six to three.

In *Bostock,* the problem at the penumbra—as big as it was—is tiny compared to the problem of abortion. There is not even a penumbra, as in *Bostock.* It ends up in the court because of the incapacity of the two houses of Congress to act. By some act of legislature or parliament, every country but ours has resolved the rules about abortion, for better or worse, but it's hard to imagine in our country that anything similar could come out of Congress. It's no more emotional or divisive here than anywhere else, but it's beyond our form of government for a legislature to resolve.

So that's why I'm a lawyer. At age twenty-two, I was smitten with the idea I could do the work of democracy and be part of this deep state without ever needing to run for an office. I could find a desk somewhere and write.

Now I have come to believe that if the legislative branch is dysfunctional, the judicial branch will be too. It will end up invading the lawmaking function of the other branch—it will end up doing what the People's House should do. Maybe with gridlock there is no choice. Yet the Warren Court was at its best in the mid- to late-1960s, when Congress was briefly functioning too. But it is too hard for the court to do a workaround of a constitution incapable of representing the people. In law school, I had high hopes because of a long-ago 1938 Supreme Court case, *Carolene Products Inc. v. United States.* Never mind the holding—approving a New Deal price support for milk. The big point—dropped in footnote four—was a declaration of a new form of judicial review. From now on, the court would leave the New Deal alone. It would only strike down laws that (1) obstruct majority rule, or (2) harm "discrete, insular minorities." Even in carrying out (2), it would be doing the work of (1). For there would be no true majority rule until everyone was included.

And so we got *Brown v. Board* and *Baker v. Carr*, which required one person, one vote in the states. I thought we could put in place a real democracy just with footnote four.

Of course, that depended on there being judges picked by elected officials who already wanted a real democracy in place. But except for that small point, what attracted me was that it was all so coherent. Say this much for judicial review of the Left: it all adds up. You knew, if you knew footnote four, where a liberal judge would come out.

On the other hand, with the conservatives who took over later—the Federalist Society, the late Justice Scalia and his many disciples—there was and still is no such coherent form of judicial review. It's all ad hoc. There is no overarching principle like footnote four to say where they will come out. Original intent? Most historians scoff. There is a whole flock of original intents. Textualism? Text is fluid. There are fifty maxims of construction, and they contradict each other. Every try by the Right at a paradigm ends up as a flop.

The strange thing is, in a way, they do have a paradigm. It's to figure out what the Left will do in footnote four and do the reverse.

If the Left promotes majority rule and incorporating discrete, insular minorities, the most predictable thing about the Right is that they will try to stop it. Unlike the liberal judges, they can't acknowledge what they are doing or figure out how to explain it.

There is not that coherence that makes the law seem lawlike. That's what most of the country has come to grasp, even if we cannot readily explain why we have that feeling. There is no lawlike rule of law. Trump had reason to think it was even worse than it was. It seemed plausible enough to him after *Bush v. Gore* that the court might stomp all over the 2020 election too. He was wrong. Here's why: it would have been the end of the world. It would have put the rule of law, and the court itself, out of business—and that is not what any of the nine justices want to do.

This was also the unspoken issue in our case before the court. It was whether Congress, on an obscure statutory question, could put the court out of business by taking away its jurisdiction to hear constitutional claims. As it turned out, it was an issue on which all nine of the justices would agree.

———————

In our case, the issue was whether Congress could use the biggest "nuclear option" of all—namely, to get rid of judicial review *altogether*. Could it just strip the court of jurisdiction to hear a constitutional claim? It's in the public debate right now: instead of just packing the court, which looks tawdry, why not pass laws that stop the court from applying the Constitution to a law like the ACA?

Or: instead of packing the court, just put it out of business. Can Congress really do that?

Now ours may have looked like a tiny minnow of a lawsuit. Our clients drove trains out in Kansas and Missouri. We were representing the Central Conference of the Brotherhood of Locomotive Engineers and Trainmen (BLET). Things had gone bad in an arbitration. The arbitrator had tossed out eight of our cases for failing to have a preliminary meeting to see if the claim could be settled. Tossed them out—based on a new rule about his "jurisdiction." So in 2008, before I ran for the House, we had filed suit in federal court to overturn the arbitrator's decision, both under the Constitution as well as federal labor law. Now, it may seem odd that we could sue under the US Constitution—it's just a labor arbitration—but here's the catch. In the railroad world, unlike the rest of the world, the arbitrator is from a federal agency, the National Railway Adjustment Board. The arbitrator *is,* technically, the federal government. So we could argue that this arbitrator—"the federal government"—had denied us the right to due process under the Fifth Amendment. We also argued that the arbitrator had violated our rights under a statute passed by Congress in 1965 to replace these claims for violation of due process. But the statute—take my word for it—did not have a category that fit what we were arguing. And in the US Court of Appeals for the Seventh Circuit—sitting in Chicago—we had won on the due process claim and not the statutory one.

We had won!

Not so fast: Union Pacific Railroad Company was on the other side. I know it is hard to believe in the age of Google and Amazon and Apple, but Union Pacific is still secretly in charge of the country. It is much bigger, maybe even more powerful than Union Pacific in the nineteenth century, when it was the biggest thing around. Sure, on Wall Street, Tesla Motors is a lot bigger than UP, but Tesla isn't moving the country, while UP is. And it's really, really big. A few years before, UP had bought up Southern Pacific Railroad, which was the Octopus in Frank Norris's 1903 novel of the same name. It had swallowed the Octopus. And its tentacles are all over the country, including

Washington, DC. Dick Cheney was on the board of directors; at the time, so was Andrew Card, just after being Bush Two's White House chief of staff. And according to a Pulitzer Prize-winning *New York Times* investigation, UP had also swallowed up the Federal Railroad Administration, if not the whole US Department of Transportation.

If Union Pacific wanted the case in the Supreme Court, it had a good chance of going up to the Supreme Court. And UP was mad at the Seventh Circuit. It hated losing. And it had one of the golden law firms, the Washington, DC, office of Latham and Watkins. The argument was simple: *Congress had gotten rid of constitutional due process.* Congress had closed the door.

Of course, Congress did not keep the court from hearing *statutory* claims; rather, as UP saw it, Congress had stopped the hearing of *constitutional* ones. When it had amended the Railway Labor Act in 1965, it had stripped the court of its power in this area to enforce the Constitution. In other words, it could put the court out of business. Since it was UP, it was likely UP would win. The court does not take a case to affirm it.

Sure, I was terrified—like a nun being summoned to the Vatican to explain herself. A friend had called: "Congratulations: you're in the Supreme Court." Or, "That should make up for losing that election." I groaned. "It's not like I wanted to be up there." A left-wing lawyer friend said, "Of course I knew you didn't want to be up there. They don't grant petitions from people like you and me." On the other hand, I was thrilled: I was going to Washington, DC; not "Washington, DC" in quotes, to which I referred above, but the real one, in DC itself. While I had never stepped inside the court, I used to haunt the Library of Congress next door. I lived in DC for most of my twenties. I might not have stepped on Olympus, but I had spent a lot of time on Parnassus. I used to sit in the dark of the reading room under those little green lamps and then get in line with a date on Friday night to get into the Coolidge Auditorium to hear the Juilliard String Quartet or some less polished chamber music group put on a concert of Schubert or Shostakovich for free. I spent my twenties going back and forth from the dark mahogany of the reading room to the dark mahogany of the violins and violas on the floor below. I fell in love with so many of the young women playing those violas and violins, in white blouses and black dresses, and it never occurred to me even once to go to the Supreme Court next door.

Now, many years later, I was to find out in the court there were women in black dresses too.

And I had an even better seat than the first row in the Coolidge Auditorium. I have tried to get this across to my fellow lawyers in Chicago: I was at eye level, six feet from the justices. OK, it's more, but I was shocked how close I was. It was more intimate than any argument I ever had in the US Court of Appeals, at least in Chicago. There, the Seventh Circuit is on the twenty-seventh floor of a scary Mies van der Rohe building, all black and glass, and the three judges on the appeals panel perch high above the lawyers, staring down from this star-chamber height. It is an early, neofuturist, fascist palace that Mussolini would have liked, and there is a near replica of the Seventh Circuit in the Bertolucci film *The Conformist,* a movie I hope never again to watch.

By comparison, the US Supreme Court is surprisingly unscary, a comparative country courthouse. For a moment, I remember thinking, "Gregory Peck playing Atticus Finch in

To Kill a Mockingbird would fit right in here." It has a Southern charm, which is scary only if you are Dred Scott, or Plessy in *Plessy v. Ferguson*, or otherwise trying to escape from whites.

And here is another surprising thing—the justices were nice. Or at least they were nice enough, or nicer than some of the judges in the Seventh Circuit. I was surprised because I had signed up for and taken a "boot camp" for first-time Supreme Court lawyers, people like me who get up there once and never again. For a lawyer who did a lot of scut work at the bottom—depositions, productions of documents, Rule Twenty-Six disclosures—I had done a decent amount of appellate argument, but I was told the Supreme Court was different. But I remember my boot camp instructor chiding me: "ANSWER MY QUESTION! I know what Justice Kennedy will do; he will just turn his chair around and stop looking at you." Really? That seemed a little childish. Maybe it's true, but it didn't happen to me.

So what is the difference between an oral argument in the Court of Appeals and one in the US Supreme Court?

Well, here's the biggest one: there are nine judges instead of three, and you know in advance who they are going to be. In the appellate courts, you don't know until 8:50 a.m. which three of the fifteen or so judges will be sitting on the panel to hear your case at 9:15 a.m. But in the case of the Supreme Court, if you are a sentient human being, you have a pretty good idea who is going to be on the bench. This is a good thing to know.

Also, with nine, the odds are good that *someone* is going to be on your side, or will at least refrain from beating you up. With just three, the odds are worse—perhaps all three of them will turn their chairs around. So given that the Supreme

Court would likely split five to four against a labor union and for an employer, I could think: "Well, maybe the four will try to protect me."

I even had the fantasy: "Maybe *all* of them would like me." To the liberal four I could say, "May it please the Court, I am a registered Democrat." And to the conservative five I could say, "May it please the Court, I am a practicing Catholic," as all five of those justices were.

I am just kidding. I was terrified. For advice, I googled the chief justice, who as a lawyer had argued many times before the court. His advice: expect to get out a sentence, only one, before the Nine come pounding down on you with questions. I kept writing out that sentence. Over and over. And over. That sentence filled up five legal pads. By a yellow candle, at a Greek restaurant the night before the case, I spilled olive oil all over me as I wrote new versions of the Sentence. Yes, I was terrified. The case was up at 1:00 p.m., when I usually take a nap. I was sure to be off, and the court would know it. I tried to remember the advice I had from a lawyer friend, Marty Schneiderman: "Try to have some fun with it." I bought a new shirt at Jos. A. Bank. What about my shoes? I raised it with Mike, my law partner. "They're brown," I said. "Won't they expect black shoes?" He stared. "They're not going to look at your shoes."

Also, I was rattled because the AFL-CIO had come out against us; yes, against a *labor union*. Oh, nominally, they said we should win on statutory grounds, but they agreed with UP that Congress had taken away the right of the railroad engineers to sue for due process.

I had pleaded with the AFL-CIO attorneys who thought the whole case was a nuisance. "If we have constitutional rights," they said, "then management will start saying *they* have constitutional rights. See? It will just be a mess."

"Wait," I said. "What lawyer would tell their clients to give up their constitutional rights?"

Well, anyway, the AFL-CIO came out against constitutional rights, as they are a lot of bother.

So the big day came, and up we trudged to our highest court. My cocounsel, Carol Nguyen, would be sitting next to me as second chair. Carol had never even seen the court or been to DC before. Thank God for her; she was unflappable and a huge help. A half hour before the case was called, someone from the clerk's office came out and gave us a tour. For ten minutes or so I was looking up at the ceiling instead of down at my notes. And as we took the tour, I kept thinking of the biggest boot camp rule of all: *Don't say your name to the court.* Like any other lawyer, I was used to giving my name: "May it please, I am blank for the blank." Not so in the Supreme Court, said the boot camp guy. "They know your name. You just say, 'May it please the Court.' But don't say your name. It's the biggest mistake that the inexperienced Supreme Court lawyer makes." I just hoped Justice Kennedy would not turn around in his chair.

The case was called and the justices came out, including the newest justice, Sonia Sotomayor, in her second day on the job. Though the lowest-ranking justice, she spoke first (or so I recall) and said more or less as follows: "We ask that counsel not address the constitutional claim but only whether the arbitrator's decision violated the statute."

Wait: the court had taken this case to determine whether Congress could eliminate the court's jurisdiction to hear constitutional claims. *Now* the court said to forget about it?

That meant I and the UP lawyer, who had been a Scalia clerk, would have to throw out three-quarters of the briefs.

Fortunately for me, UP was up first. While he argued, I had a half hour or so to collect my thoughts. It turns out I was so overprepared that on what was left to argue, I still could have talked for five days.

When the UP lawyer sat down, I was ready to go. The chief justice nodded and said, "And now we will hear from Mr . . ."

He paused. "Mr . . ."

How I knew that pause from law school, when my teachers would look down to find my name on the seating chart and stop.

"Mr . . ."

I had no choice but to throw boot camp out the window.

"It's . . . Geoghegan," I said. I could have added: it rhymes with Reagan. But with this court, it might have seemed to be pandering.

The chief justice seemed to smile; it had been OK to break the rule.

As to the oral argument, I had a half hour to talk directly to the gods, with nothing but the starry sky above. Of course, I loved it. No justice swiveled their chair around to show their contempt. The liberal justices had pounded on the UP lawyer. The conservatives had their chance with me. But not a peep from a single justice about the constitutional claim: it was weird. When I sat down, Carol sent me a note: "We have Scalia." I thought, Oh, come on. She said a few minutes later, "I'm telling you, we have Scalia." Then the justices rose. *All rise.* I turned around and saw my Uncle Bill.

"Your father would have been proud of you," he said.

I—I . . . I forgot where I was.

My uncle himself had argued a case in the Supreme Court. He had the same reaction as I did to that tour of the building:

"Why don't I come back and do this another time?"

A lawyer friend, Marty Schneiderman, had said, "Try to have some fun with it." I did. Except for Carol, everyone thought we had lost. But I did have fun. When I stood up there I thought, "I have thirty minutes—so in a half hour, this is over, forever." There will be no more nights alone, in Greek restaurants, writing the Sentence over and over.

Of course, to this day, I have no memory of what I did say. But it was over! You get a quill pen from the clerk like it is the state fair, and you never have to think about it again.

And I had been close enough to see why a justice might hang on to such a wonderful job. Ruth Bader Ginsburg that month had just come out of chemotherapy. Her husband had just died. She looked awful, though she was lively and asked questions. If I had thought about it—and I didn't—I would have said she wasn't going to make it. But she went on for ten more years. Yes, it's an incredible job. Better than being US president. Instead of two terms, a justice is there for life. A president can only propose a law. A justice can rewrite the Constitution. No one bothers justices. There is no dialing for dollars, as the poor House members across the street were doing at that moment. There is no getting up at 6:00 a.m. to stand outside the El. "Oh, but you're just one of Nine." Exactly. You will never get all the blame for any one decision.

It's more than there being nothing between you as a judge and the starry sky above, as Oliver Wendell Holmes Jr. put it in *The Common Law* (1881). It's the power to put a new star up there. Indeed, they are the stars. In a real democracy, we would not even know their names: in the UK or Germany, well-informed citizens would struggle to name even one judge on their highest court. In the case of our presidents, it's the one lasting achievement they always cite: "I named a justice to the court."

We may have a true democracy only when—with majority rule—we are unable to name even a single justice on the court.

But some citizens can name them all, or five of them at least, without being able to name more than five members of the US House.

Had I thought about it while I was arguing—and I sure didn't—I would have felt sorry for members of the House. Why had I tried to get in? This was so much better. While I was arguing that afternoon, they—maybe all 435 of them—were probably running like little ants across the street to answer the bell before the vote. Then back across the street they would skitter to do their little cold calls for money. If I had been in the US House, I would never be done. Even Marjorie Taylor Greene is never done.

After the oral argument was finished, I went to a Capitol Hill bar with Carol, Mike, our clients Ronnie and Kyle, and a bunch of others and did what I never do—downed cocktails without food. I was done! I had gotten out the Sentence, even if I could not remember what it was. I remember that a manager from Union Pacific—not a lawyer—had come up to me and was smiling after we had argued. "Well," he said, "I guess everything really is five to four." And I, too, and everyone else in the bar were sure that we had lost. Hey, it's not our fault: it was always going to be five to four.

And it is scary to think now that we had in fact won, nine to zero.

I must mention the saddest thing. The BLET chairman, Charlie Rightnowar, had been too sick to come. He had been the heart and soul of this case. He might have been the best client I ever had. So how did I get him? I am not sure. A few years back he had retained our firm for a few cases. I wondered, "Why did he come to us?"

After we had finished talking business in that first hour, he paused and said, "Now, Tom, I'd like to ask you—what do you think of Noam Chomsky?"

I am still unsure why he had picked our firm, but his doing so is why we ended up in the Supreme Court.

When I saw the House Office Building later that evening, with those tiny offices crammed with interns sitting on top of each other, and the buffet hour starting on the ground floor, the story about Bernie and Mike came to mind. When Bernie was thinking of running for the US House, he went to his friend Mike, who was in Congress. Would he like doing it?

Mike said, "You think you're up to it? Going out every night, eating that plastic banquet food, or off buffets, always raising money, never any time for yourself—think you're able to live like that?"

Bernie said, "Well, how are you able to do it?"

"Me?" said Mike. "I love it!

I might have come to love it, even after 2010 when the GOP took over the Congress. But even then, I would have been dialing for dollars to keep myself in the House minority. I would have been up on a bike in the House gym, maybe even by 4:00 a.m. like poor old Chuck Grassley.

Yes, the House was about to flip, but I possibly would have been elected for life, and I could not stop just because the GOP was in. And as the democracy darkened and became ungovernable, and as the divide seemed to become deeper and darker, nothing could be done but to be up on the bike—and just to keep pedaling faster and faster.

CHAPTER THREE:
FOCUS ON LABOR, NOT MORE COLLEGE

After 2010, the House did flip. It was still a battering ram, but it had no interest in battering anything but Obama. It seems impossible for the House ever to be controlled by the GOP; for it to be so is to be estranged from itself. It is to violate its nature as the People's House.

It's awful to think that I might have had to sit there helpless while at the desk next to me, a member of the Freedom Caucus screamed. House members in those years were trying out the kind of lines that Trump would later tweet. In those years, they were going from the House floor to Fox News, and then from Fox back to the House, and it is not just Fox but the House itself as the People's House that corrupted the people. Of course, it is impossible to know what part of the conditioning came from the House and what came from Fox. But the House being the House, it was like a thermometer that gave us a reading as to how feverish and ill the country was becoming.

I had years to relish being clobbered in that election. My attempt to get to Washington had reintroduced me to Chicago. Like many in that awful time, I flourished as a local citizen—because it was so depressing nationally.

For example, I filed a civil rights suit to stop the mayor (our old friend Rahm Emanuel) from closing fifty-three public schools and at least saved four of them. I filed a suit to stop

George Lucas from building a Star Wars museum on Lake Michigan—and received an award that I was a Jedi warrior. Yet even as a reborn local citizen, I kept one big national cause—to bring back a labor movement. It was a strange thing to be on the left and fighting the good fight for people who would vote for Trump.

Meanwhile, until 2016, we had a president who with style and grace could still hold off the Right. When I love him so much this is a hard thing to say, but after 2010, when even the House was lost, a kind of decadence descended on us. There was nothing we could do, but we could tell ourselves that Obama could hold them off.

It was best not to think that one day Obama would be gone.

In a used bookstore the other night, I found a copy of *Strange Defeat* by the great medieval historian Marc Bloch, written in 1940—in hiding, in the Resistance—while the French army was not just crushed, but waiting to be crushed. Bloch, who had been a brave officer, took pains to show that even before the Germans came, the war, in a sense, was already over.

There is a masterpiece of irony called "Waiting for the Barbarians," a poem by C. P. Cavafy. The shock of its last lines is that the barbarians never come, or even exist. And it's a shame, because for an empire that had lost its nerve, it would have been a kind of solution.

The Trump Era was—in a way—a kind of solution. It was the end of the decadence of the Obama Era, when we expected Obama alone to hold off the barbarians. But the election of Trump, and then the defeat of him in 2020, helped us to recover our nerve. The Democratic Party has today acquired a determination that I have never known it to have before.

Maybe it will even become a party that brings back the working class. Or maybe it will come to nothing. Maybe we are changing as a party only so everything can stay the same. Or maybe something big is in store. As Zhou Enlai famously said when asked what he thought about the French Revolution, "It's too soon to tell."

It is too soon to tell—but that's no reason to hold off a book.

Trump may have been the only presidential candidate ever to trigger two landslides, one for and one against him. There was no bigger spur to the fury of one landslide than the fury of the other. I admit: I never dreamed Trump would get ten million more votes in 2020 than in 2016 despite the pandemic. Or maybe, in some twisted way, he got them because of the pandemic? The lie is that on Election Day, the Democrats found just enough votes to win. But closer to the truth—or a figurative one—is that Republicans had to come up with enough in-person votes to match the mail-in ballots that had come pouring in from (largely) Democrats. The act of watching, helpless, as that mail-ballot majority rolled in had an uncanny way of calling out an in-person majority to cancel it out.

Of course it was not enough. Trump did lose by seven million votes. Yet many a polling place was real estate which the white working class on Election Day stormed and occupied, like a general strike. And no matter how preposterous Trump's lie about election fraud was, there must be a rage, and maybe a lasting rage, that such an immediate and strenuous show be canceled out by such an intangible one.

And it may also add to Trump's appeal: the appeal of being the rejected one, a misfit, made to order in a country where more and more working people feel they have no role to play.

At least the Democrats, for the first time in my life, now have a leader in Biden who comes across as a regular guy. But we have an even bigger challenge—after Trump's turnout—to call ourselves a working-class party.

Here's a little thought experiment: What would happen if, by a snap of the fingers, white racism in America disappeared? It might be that the Black and Latino working class would then be voting for Trump and the GOP too. Some already started doing so in the 2020 election. We on the left often tell ourselves, "Oh, we lost just the white working class because of race." But the truth might be something closer to this: "It's only because of race that we have any part of the working class turning out for us at all."

How many in the party's postgraduate base have even a single friendship, a real one of two equals, with any man or woman who is just a high school graduate? Try to imagine a Democrat in either the House or the Senate without a college degree. Maybe that's an unfair thing to say. Still, it's unthinkable that the college-educated base of the party would trust a high school graduate without a four-year degree to hold a serious office. We would never vote for them. Why should they ever vote for one of us?

It used to be otherwise. Yes, in the 1940s and 1950s, many a Democrat in the House or Senate had no four-year diploma. Even the president, Harry Truman, did not. What's more, those who did typically went to night law school or a teachers' college and at least still lived, or had a social life, in neighborhoods where no one over a long stretch of city blocks had college degrees. This was true even for the profession now cited as a sort of polemic shorthand for rule by the knowledge elite—the "liberal media." As late as

1970, my friend Steve Franklin joined a city paper and was surprised to learn that most of the editors had never been to college—and of course they lived in neighborhoods all over the city with people who had gone to the same high schools they had.

Back then, many of these people understood that they could trust the Democratic Party for the same reason they could trust the liberal media. The Democratic Party of the 1950s and 1960s was probably much more corrupt and inept than the Democratic Party today, but back then *it lived in the neighborhood*. It no longer does today. Now the Democratic Party relies on think tanks at elite universities to find out what people back in those neighborhoods are thinking.

In fact, the college graduates who are now the Democratic base have moved working people out of the old neighborhoods. I think here of my own city, where the members of the city council, whom columnists from Ben Hecht to Mike Royko used to mock, now have more degrees than Hecht or Royko ever would. Here's the finding of a new study from the University of Chicago at Illinois (UIC): in 1970, *one half* of Chicago was "middle income"—that is to say, the people who made up the old working-class machine vote—without four-year college degrees. Now that "middle income" group is just 16 percent. The bungalows in those formerly middle-income, high-school-graduate neighborhoods now belong to tech entrepreneurs and investors in hedge funds.

That was the whole fantasy of my run for the House: as a labor lawyer, I would bridge the divide. I imagined TV ads: "He got a pension for my dad." It was all vanity. One of the biggest things I learned in running for office was that the working class had moved away—from me, literally—on a far bigger scale than the *New York Times* or public policy journals had led me to believe.

Yes, I still tried to find and drop in on twenty-four-hour grills, and even tried a video with me talking to a waitress, and it seemed like the kind of thing that once did happen in our office. But I was embarrassed doing it. I had no idea how the old working class of Chicago had disappeared like the Etruscans. I had looked at all those precincts west of the Kennedy, where we had put our campaign office in a converted beauty parlor, the only blue-collar location not too far from a Starbucks (I wanted to be near "my" base). And I did see, once or twice, an old guy with an apron selling the *Sun-Times*, as if time had stopped in 1952. But if not gone, the working class I saw was more threadbare and lower income than the working class that used to elect candidates from the Machine. Of course, I should have known: I should not have needed monographs to tell me. The people left here in place of an older and prouder and wealthier working class no longer expected to decide who would represent the Fifth.

Years later, we have elected a mayor, Lori Lightfoot, and what astonishes is not that she is a woman, or Black, or LGBT, as there are other local politicians like her, but rather that she is so totally from out of town: not born here, never went to high school or college here, or even somewhere in the state. She showed up for the first time for law school at the University of Chicago, a place that did not even count as being Chicago when I moved here. Her election had yet to happen, but already when I was running, what was left here of the working class may have started to lose heart.

It should not be necessary to call upon the French to explain what was right in front of my nose. But this fits the claim French geographer Christophe Guilluy makes about his own country in his book *Twilight of the Elites: Prosperity, the Periphery, and the Future of France* (2017). Guilluy describes the movement, if not the expulsion, of the working class from France's most prosperous cities incubating the innovation and new modes of production that fuel the growth of the knowledge economy. The same thing is happening in places like Chicago and most of the other well-off and innovative capitals of information-age enterprise. Alexis de Tocqueville blamed the French Revolution in part on just the literal physical distance between an aristocracy pulled into Versailles and the rural France they left behind. Now, those of us with postgraduate degrees live in our own Versailles, and we don't know any working-class people either—except perhaps those who work for us.

For those of us cut off from the white working class, it is easy to think the answer to inequality is: *Imitate us.* Why can't they be like we are? I borrow this idea from *The Light that Failed: A Reckoning,* by Stephen Holmes and Ivan Krastev (2019), a book that explains why formerly Communist countries turned away from being liberal democracies to becoming authoritarian or illiberal ones. *Imitate us*—be like we are—turns out to be one of the most grating forms of foreign policy on offer in a world of such great income inequality. But *imitate us* is also grating within a country with income inequality on the scale even of France, much less that of the United States. There are other geopolitical reasons beyond my ken for the rise of Putin in Russia and Orban in Hungary, but there is something about *imitate us* that helps account both for the rise of these forms of illiberal democracy and the one that's been hatched here.

For years, the Center-Left and Progressive Left—or the postgraduates who control both sides in the party's debate—had a similar answer to inequality. Higher taxes on the wealthy? Yes. More welfare for the poor? Yes. And for everyone else? More college; a lot more college.

What to do about the lack of mobility? More college. What about competing in the global economy? More college.

If a few have started to detect the class snobbery here and added community college, it's still . . . well, it's still in the hope more people will go to college. And yes, I know; we are living increasingly in a knowledge- and data-driven economy, managed by credentialed and accomplished symbolic analysts. So to them it's obvious. How can the answer *not* be education?

Well, of course education *should* be the answer—but it *will be* the answer only when it becomes a democratic education for a democratic workplace in a country that has a more democratic form of government than our own.

It is true that Biden remarkably did not embrace college for all, but Sanders and Warren and many other candidates did. And if college for all is muted thanks to the immediate crisis created by the pandemic, it is still the core belief of the Democratic Party that now has its base within a highly educated elite. How could it not be? It's what worked for them. It's what the party leaders hear when they call up for money. "I think the real answer is education." "Let me put it in one word: education." It's unfair to blame Obama, Kerry, or Gore because it is so often what they heard.

For the base of the Democratic Party, there is nothing wrong with liberal meritocracy that more meritocracy cannot fix. It is the answer to everything. *Imitate us*—the helicopter parents, whose parents were professionals, whose candidates are Rhodes Scholars or presidents of the *Harvard Law Review*. Can college for all solve the problems of this country? Well, it worked for us. Even some of the Social Darwinists were subtler in rubbing it in.

And there are now politicians—and even an occasional professor or two, like Michael Sandel—urging us to tone it down. But even if we tone it down, many a Trump voter is right to think it really is what we believe. And it is hypocrisy just to tone it down if the so-called party of the working class cannot offer a different form of education for a different kind of workplace.

I hate to pick on Barack Obama because I genuinely like him and admire his legacy. But let me cite his famous speech on inequality, at Osawatomie, Kansas, where Theodore Roosevelt as a Bull Moose candidate had once given a tirade on inequality. It's here where, at last, Obama first acknowledged income inequality as the defining issue of the time. But what did a white working class hear as the president's number one solution to the scourge hollowing out communities and life prospects in dying factory towns and communities? He said, "We've got to up our game. . . . It starts by making education a national mission—a national mission. (Applause) . . . In this economy a higher education is the surest way to the middle class."

The White House website made the mandate even starker as it played up the president's speech: "Earning a post-secondary degree or credential is no longer just a pathway to opportunity for a talented few, rather it is a prerequisite for the growing jobs of the new economy."

Imitate us. And that's the Center-Left. Farther left it gets worse. Bernie Sanders has a bill captioned "College for All." That's *all*, as in "everyone." I regret that even Elizabeth

Warren, my ideal of a presidential candidate, has signed on. I gave money to her campaign! Of course, she is just reflecting what so many highly educated Democrats think.

I used to despair: does anyone in the Democratic Party get it? It seems that for the first time in my adult lifetime, the current president does. But do the rest of us get it? *This is a high school nation.* Even now, after all the years of pumping up college education as the only way to survive, close to 70 percent of US adults from age twenty-four to sixty-four—yes, living right now—don't have four-year college degrees. If higher education is the only way to survive in a global economy, then the party's answer, in effect, to the working class—white, Black, and Latino too—is "too late for you."

If FDR is not rolling over in his grave, Harry Truman is. Liberals talk like this as if people with high school degrees were not in the room. Who in the GOP would go to a NASCAR rally and talk about there being no hope without a four-year degree?

No wonder so many flip us the finger. In 2016, it was political genius for Trump to say, "I love the poorly educated." And it was also genius for Trump to make a point of pumping up his own moral squalor. He invites his supporters to be as much of a misfit as he is. And even if most do not take up that invitation and would never go as far at the Proud Boys or Oath Keepers or Rudy Giuliani, at least they have the opportunity at last to vote for a presidential candidate who is incapable of looking down on them.

Yes, there's race and immigration and globalization to scare the white working class, but there's something even scarier and harder for the party of the Left to address. It's the knowledge economy, which belongs to the postgraduate elite. It's the human capital, which the elite hoard—even in the act of mating, with JDs, MDs, PhDs, and hedge fund managers all marrying each other—and which we cannot imagine sharing with people who didn't even go to college. There should be a Gini index to measure inequality in human capital as we measure it in wealth. In that sense, the vote for Trump is the Luddite equivalent of taking a hammer to smash that human capital on which everything in the future will run. The turnout for Trump in 2020 put us on notice that the white working class sees what is happening. Parts of the Black and Latino working class may break off and join them.

It's true that more than half of high school graduates now go on to college. But it's also true that this is why we have so many dropouts, people who *tried* to imitate us and now carry so much shame and debt. It's hard to think of a better way of creating a social explosion.

The whole postgraduate project defies logic or reason. That increase in the number of graduates that we are likely to get—those additional ones at the margin, as an economist might like to say—will be not just in nursing or law enforcement, but business administration.

And what do these extra college graduates with these business degrees do? They supervise the working class—all of it, white, Black, and Brown. In other words: a college education is valuable to the extent that other people are not getting one. But of course, we're not supposed to think about such a thing.

Still, let's think about it anyway. The more people we force into college, the more the class that has a stake in pumping up the college premium, or the increment over what working-class people get, becomes correspondingly more powerful.

That is, the more this class has to invest in themselves by going to college, the more they will want to see a college premium, a return on their investment, at least for the time they spend out of the workforce. That's the class we're building up. *That* class—the one even the Hard Left itself is trying to build up—has no stake in letting the high school graduates do anything to decrease that premium. The more Obama and you and I tout college, the more we are committed to the project of pushing up that premium to justify a college education and making the life prospects of working people even worse.

In other words, with the best of intentions, we end up screwing them. It is what, in the old days, Marxists would call an ideology—until Marxists in our own time began pushing college for all. And we don't expect a blowback?

Of course we should have more college, and it should be cheaper, if not free. But more college should be part of a new and more democratic education that reflects a new and more democratic workplace. There are many examples in Europe; I urge people to read the work of scholars like Kathleen Thelen at MIT and others. Among these alternative European capitalisms, Denmark is still the gold standard. In Denmark, there is commitment to education at all levels, at all points of life. It is a system where the state makes a heavy investment in training that makes no distinctions and eliminates boundaries; it is the same commitment to training for the employed and the unemployed, for white-collar and blue-collar, for college graduate and high school graduate, for those early in life and those midcareer. It is not our idea of job training—to fit people into a narrow occupational role. It is continued training in social and communication skills for a knowledge- and service-based economy.

It would be wonderful to have it here. But this lifetime learning is more likely to work in a society that is already as egalitarian as Denmark in the first place. In a sense, we have to get to Denmark before we can be like Denmark.

I admit to being much influenced by a recent book by Branko Milanović, *Capitalism, Alone: The Future of the System That Rules the World* (2019). Milanović is a former World Bank economist and appears to be well-connected with the elite and powerful. He has a particular critique of liberal meritocratic capitalism, which in the US had replaced the much more social democratic capitalism of the post-New Deal. For Milanović, the challenge is to lessen the huge inequality in our form of capitalism—both in terms of human and financial capital. For human capital, it requires improving public education, and for financial capital, it especially requires much heavier estate taxation.

In the case of K–12 public education, underfunded as it is, the problem may be worse than Milanović says. It arises from a new standards-based movement in public education, which is in principle a good thing. In forty-one states and the District of Columbia, students are now assessed every year under the Common Core standards put in place by state law. Of course it's good—low-income students in poor districts get cheated when they are not held to higher standards. Yet many rural white children and minority children live in school districts that do not have the capacity to educate their students to meet the standards.

That is just what has happened in my own state, Illinois. Right now, our tiny firm, in another overreach, I fear, is about to argue a case in the Illinois Supreme Court to establish a constitutional right to funding of the Common

Core standards. I should say: it's the constitution of Illinois, not the United States. We represent twenty-two poor or low-wealth downstate Illinois school districts—far south of Chicago in the reddest part of our very blue state. And our claim is simple: we want the state to kick in enough money to give these twenty-two districts the resources to prepare their students to pass the exams. There is now in place a state law that determines need based on what is called "evidence-based funding." Without going into detail, this formula—the state's own formula—estimates that all the low-wealth districts, including the twenty-two we represent, need an additional $7.2 billion in annual aid to give students in those districts a chance to meet the standards that will determine their future—college or community college or nothing.

Now imagine that you are a student, low-income or just in a low-wealth district, in that part of Illinois that people are abandoning. Every year you might well be one of the many who are branded by the state as a failure, or at least as failing to meet standards—even though it may be the state's own fault. Then, under state law, there is a final assessment that goes into your so-called "permanent" record: that's the failure to meet standards that can never be erased. And it's small comfort to know that your school, for lack of resources, is not meeting standards either.

Illinois is bad, to be sure, but at least it's a blue state. Other states are even worse. All across the country right now, we are branding working-class kids as failures, and placing it in their permanent records, because we are not willing to pay enough in taxes for them to succeed.

Now try to imagine the rage when the society in which you are trying to shape an identity has placed failure in your record—

and then told you that your only hope is to go to college.

Yet lest we extend too much compassion to the students and their families, I may as well note that in 2020, these same people largely voted against a progressive income tax that might have paid for that extra annual $7.2 billion. It may be hard to convince the Illinois Supreme Court to opt for spending that the white working class itself in downstate Illinois just voted down. No doubt by the time this book comes out, we will have lost.

Still, while $7.2 billion is a figure unique to Illinois, it gives a sense of the shortfall across the land. At least in the old days, the inequality may have been bad, but the state itself was not placing a brand upon your head.

Maybe being a labor lawyer I push the point too far, but if we really believed in education and wanted to create democracy in the schools and inch working-class children toward equal footing with children of the elite, we might at least think about democracy in the workplace. It's a point made by that great liberal philosopher and educator John Dewey—by whom, in a book I wrote once, I became so transfixed. **It is the view that there can be no democracy in education unless there is democracy at work. If we really wanted to improve public education and make our liberal meritocracy more liberal and less meritocratic, we would start with labor law reform, or in some way create a more democratic workplace.**

———————

Dewey's point was underscored years ago by Mary Douglas, the great cultural anthropologist. In her book *Natural Symbols*, she was one of the first to describe the difference in the way professional-class parents and working-class parents raise their children.

Working-class people in this country are stuck in authoritarian workplaces and learn to take orders—and they raise their children in that way too. As Douglas writes, they are simply told that this is how things are, much the way their parents are told at work. In her typology, these children grow up as prisoners of a speech code—what she and others call, perhaps awkwardly, "condensed speech." By contrast, the children of the postgraduates and professionals are encouraged to inquire, and because their parents have a sense of agency, their children are more likely to get answers—not in condensed, but elongated speech codes. If children grow up with these condensed speech codes, which come from parents with no sense of agency or control over their lives, it will take a lot more money than $7.2 billion for schools to counteract that effect. Or we can educate our young much better to the extent that their parents get to dabble once in a while in elongated speech codes at work. The more democracy there is, the easier it is to educate children in the skills to participate in a democracy. At least the state itself is not branding them as failures.

But is that really true? Well, countries with more democratic workplaces than our own are more likely to have higher class mobility, too, and those with more authoritarian workplaces like our own trap generation after generation with no way out. Until we have democracy in the workplace, there will not be democracy in education. And until that happens, there is a future for politicians like Trump who say, "I love the poorly educated." People will be looking for a way to lift their shame.

The other day I met a friend, Dick Longworth, who had found a copy of a book—*The End of Economic Man* by Peter Drucker, the famous economist, who wrote it in 1939 before he fled Hitler to live in Vienna. Drucker argued that people who supported Hitler and other fascists were tired of rational politics because rationality, whether in a liberal or Marxist form, had failed. It was the Great Depression: everything had collapsed. The thrill of fascism, or authoritarianism, Drucker argued, was precisely that it was so loopy, so counter to reason, at a moment when reason and rationality had failed. "Isn't that what is happening now?" Longworth asked.

Well, he is right, as usual, but I think there is a difference. Back in the Depression, the Enlightenment had indeed failed. Now, however, it's working only too well. The Enlightenment is coming to take away your job. Or it's poised to take away you, altogether—your moral status, your sense of self-worth, your understanding of where you belong in a feverishly globalized grid of knowledge as social power.

And all this is threatening because, as was the case during the Industrial Revolution, there is a new kind of economic order, one leading to a knowledge economy. That's the threat for so many people displaced or otherwise made redundant by the ascendancy of the postgraduate class. And that's what the Democrats at least appear to be speeding up.

But the real threat is something else: we aren't speeding it up at all. We are keeping it in the hands of a few. We don't trust the working class to have a share in it.

In his 1944 classic, *The Great Transformation,* Karl Polyani made this argument about the Industrial Revolution: it was not the material but the moral inequality that was the worst part of it. Indeed, in a material sense, the industrial workers forced into the cities were better off. Perhaps it is not economic inequality but moral inequality that is, to quote Obama, the defining issue of our time. It is the loss of social standing, social claims, the social assets that working people used to have, because in our time education is so much more decisive. Working-class constituencies have especially lost their standing in the Democratic Party, in part because many do not share our moral concerns or our own enlightened values, like open-border immigration. And Democrats rub it in—celebrate this dispossession—because as the party of education, we are the party that makes working people feel bad about themselves.

In this sense, Trump's election was a good thing. It made many of us better people; that is, committed to decency, indeed, to Enlightenment values. But it's also made us worse—quicker to brand members of the white working class as failures—and in doing so, consciously or unconsciously, we are becoming much less sympathetic to their inability to defend or safeguard their social standing in an age when higher education is everything. We also make it harder, in our carefully concealed contempt, for people not already admitted to the charmed circle of Enlightenment belonging to go on believing in themselves.

There is no foothold left in big cities, or anyplace else where the global winners live, for high-school graduates to exercise even a tiny bit of power. There's no church to slot into as a deacon, no chance on the shop floor to rise as a foreman, no union in which to become a shop steward or officeholder, no big city political machine that, in this digital age, needs anyone to go door-to-door. Our wage workers have been stripped of every way to exercise the kind of morality or to have the opportunities that come so easily to the top fifth.

At least in the case of the Industrial Revolution, as described by E. P. Thompson in *The Making of the English Working Class,* there was religion—the new Methodist faith that gave the English working class a sense of moral superiority over their owners. But in the working class that has been remade and discarded for the postindustrial age, there is an uptick in drug abuse, one-parent families, and indebtedness. The top fifth of the country, the most educated, may well be more moral—and God knows, even more religious in terms of actual Christian value—than the current white working class. But that, too, represents just another form of class oppression, worse than in the Industrial Revolution. The top fifth have appropriated all the morality.

And at least the old English working class were at the cutting edge of a new kind of economy, a new means of production. They were the advance guard in this respect, ahead of everyone else. They did enjoy—or at least must have felt—a sense of power. But in the time of Trump, this is the class that is left behind. Their real *cri de coeur*—so I would argue—is not against "globalization," or even automation, but against their own receding sense of importance in the world. In this ever-mushrooming economy that is replacing the old one, in which knowledge is power and data governs all, working people are being told they are superfluous.

They're not the advance guard of *this* revolution, the one putting in place a new type of production—the so-called knowledge economy. To the contrary, they're being kept out of it, even as they are told that we are all anxious that they be in it. They're not just making less; they're made to think they are *worth* less for not taking up an invitation that is not really being given to them.

I admit here, I am much taken by the argument of Roberto Unger's *The Knowledge Economy*. In his view, while we may claim to tout the knowledge economy, we resist letting in working-class people. After all, the more people who have a role in it, the more there are who have to be paid off. And the more that working-class people have to be paid off, the less of a payday for managers at the top. So all our touting of the knowledge economy, like college for all, is a perfect example of what French existentialists like to call "bad faith."

No wonder so many working-class people might well tell us to take our little Pell Grant program and stick it up our permanent record.

CHAPTER FOUR:
MAKE EVERYONE VOTE

M aybe the answer is in Whitman's poem "Crossing Brooklyn Ferry"—that embrace of all of us living now and those who follow us in the future. The speaker looks into the faces of travelers on that ferry and sees what I think I almost saw as a candidate when I looked at people on the El.

I am trying to think of all the bonds between us, without thinking too much of the people who voted for Trump and whom I would like to rope and tie. It all seems so naive now. We are two countries, and for at least the foreseeable future, that's the way it will be.

But there is another divide which gets little attention, and if we can overcome *that* divide, we may solve the one that is tearing apart the country. I mean forcing everyone, yes, everyone to get on the Brooklyn Ferry—the third, or half, or more than half of the electorate that in our biennial elections sit it out and just let the rest of us vote.

Yes, I am in favor of compulsory voting as the only way to settle once and for all whether we are all in this together. With all our checks and balances of our gridlocked form of government, it's only by all of us turning out in every major election that the republic can survive.

Yes, I know the official position of the Left is that everyone should vote, but it is natural that we only want to bring in those who are on our side. During the Trump presidency, with its goose-stepping right-wing nationalism, some on the left tried to offer a version of liberal nationalism. But here is where I confess that the idea of liberal nationalism puts me on edge. In my parochial grade school, I read in our civics book in fourth grade:

Patriotism is a virtue.

Nationalism is a sin.

I still think it is, albeit venial in some cases, mortal in others. What bothers me is that nationalism has to exclude, and there is at least some reason for the white working class and the dispossessed of all races to think that diversity and inclusion doesn't include them.

We need to find a better word. I think there's a word for it in Whitman; not in his poetry but in his great prose work, *Specimen Days*. It's in a note Whitman wrote about Lincoln after his assassination:

> Not but that he had faults, and show'd them in the Presidency; but honesty, goodness, shrewdness, conscience, and (a new virtue, unknown to other lands, and hardly yet really known here, but the foundation and tie of all, as the future will grandly develop,) UNIONISM, in its truest and amplest sense, form'd the hard-pan of his character.

Maybe, UNIONISM should form the hard-pan of our own. For Lincoln, UNIONISM was a commitment not just to diversity or inclusion, but to charity toward all, to a UNION even with those who wanted no part of it or us— for Lincoln, that meant not just the secessionists but all the Copperheads, who are thriving now in the north and who, at least in 2016, flipped Midwest states to Trump. UNIONISM was a commitment to what Whitman would call an "adhesive relationship." It's different from nationalism, right or left. To the extent that nationalism excludes, it puts the UNION at risk, because the UNION is quite a different thing from the nation. The UNION requires of us works and not grace—and the most important work is to pull into it even the nonvoters who would just as soon be left alone.

What does Lincoln's UNIONISM demand now, in structural terms? Well, until everyone votes, we can't have majority rule, because no majority in a low-turnout election can be regarded as legitimate.

Even in 2020, which saw an astonishing two-thirds of the vote-eligible population turn out, it was still a turnout that was, with our level of education, much lower than many other wealthy countries. That extraordinary turnout was a medium to low turnout by global standards. And that is plenty of reason for whoever loses to be suspicious, and for every election to be regarded as illegitimate.

But a Whitman-like nuclear option of compulsory voting would do away with any taint of illegitimacy. It gets to the heart of UNIONISM—being accountable to each other for how we are governed. It may also be the only way, once and for all, to end this debate now raging in red state legislatures over how much democracy the democracy should have. With compulsory voting, we end that debate by pulling in even the politically challenged. Or as Dr. Quentin Young would say about single-payer healthcare: "Everyone in, nobody out."

They're in, whether they like it or not. For if we do not end this divide between those who are in and those who are out, there is even less hope of bridging the divide between the hard-core voters.

By the way, I'm also in favor of labor law reform as a way of ending the divide, but since I can't push that in every chapter, I will just limit myself here to compulsory voting. Not just for those who are likely Democratic persons—not just for African Americans or Latinos or for the poor of every race—but for all citizens of this country, including those who are likely GOP or Trump voters. Let the Democratic Party be the party of UNION, the party of civic values. Universal suffrage by compulsion: my one big idea. Charity toward all requires a structure.

———————

In my case, it is charity toward all—but also an act of personal revenge. I have nursed it since I went as a candidate door-to-door. For every door I knocked on, I used to pass five without knocking because the poll sheets told us to knock only on the doors of the hardest-core voters. To be sure, I loved those people: we were thrilled to see each other. But my heart became bitter as I thought of the others. If I was out here risking an early death to be their House member for life, the least that they could do is to show up and vote.

Yes, it was their fault if the winning candidate had only 12,000 votes to represent 700,000 people. It was a giant flip of the finger by the people to the people running for the People's House. As glad as I was when Election Day came and the whole thing would be over, I became depressed after the initial morning "rush," if that's the right term for the few who showed up. The turnout may have been lower because a blizzard the Sunday before had made it impossible to do last-minute door-to-door visits. Then, as a kind of insult, Election Day itself, all day, was fine; no long underwear or any of that. It was maddening. There was nothing I could do as a candidate except to mope around and get in the staff's way.

One of the staff suggested, "You want to do something? Here's a call sheet. Call the names on here and ask if they have voted. And if they say yes, ask if they voted for you."

I winced. "Wait—I'm going to ask them if they voted for *me*? That's . . . like, none of my business, is it?" I could imagine people slamming down the phone or, worse, saying, "No, you asshole, I didn't vote for you." My brother came by to get me out of the office—someone probably called him. We drove out to drop leaflets in a part of the Fifth District I had never seen. We agreed to separate and meet later. But it was so suburb-like, with none of the grid-like Chicago perpendicular streets, that I soon was lost, and it took an hour for my brother to find me. Every house I passed looked empty. Even the hard-core voters were off at work. I should have been at work. In midafternoon, out here in the sunshine, I felt more like a fool than I did later when we got the results.

That morning, when I looked down the call sheet with the names of the hard-core voters, I saw what a closed little world the union had become. With our call sheets and canvassing and phoning, we leave out in any given election up to half the people or more; by design, it is not government of or by or for the people, but by, for, and of the people who, conditioned like lab rats, go to the polls and vote. Or, as in 2020—terrified for their lives—they vote by mail. It's all about turnout, and it's all about the diehards who vote in election after election. Not only do these privileged people start out by assuming voting as the norm for all sorts of reasons, but we keep reinforcing that norm throughout their lives. With our millions, or rather billions, we keep after "them," that rump electorate. In my special election, all fourteen candidates kept calling the same virtuous people over and over. They must have heard by phone from each of us at least once, or even twice, and what was even more jaw-dropping—they were often happy to get the calls. At least that's what I found, and I was on the phone a lot. I had a script.

"Pardon me, I know you're busy, but do you have a minute to hear my pitch?" I'd wait. I'd think: it's 6:00 p.m. and I bet they're cooking dinner. They're going to blow me off. No, wait for it.

"OK. Go ahead."

They never said no, except maybe if they were on the way to the hospital. "It restores your faith in humanity," one staffer said to me once as we went door-to-door. Does it? The way they said yes actually made me sad. It's the diehards who keep getting reinforced in their good democratic habits, while the others, left alone, become more isolated and disengaged. It's not just that we are unable to rule ourselves, or that we do not have a Whitman-type democracy, but we don't even have a representative government, such as Madison himself imagined, because the majority of the have-not class, or the debtor class, or the high school graduates, simply do not cast a vote. I know the answer: that's their business, not our business. But it is our business, the union's business, when they decide to sit it out and keep the Constitution from functioning.

———

As long as a third, or sometimes more than half, of people sit out the House vote, it will be impossible for the people to have a People's House. Indeed, it's been a problem for decades. But for a few accidental intervals, gridlock or dysfunctional government has been the norm. Before this present moment in the Biden presidency, I can think of only two times when the Democrats had true, gridlock-free power: between 1934 and 1938, when, by no coincidence, Congress enacted Social Security, the Wagner Act, and the Fair Labor Standards Act of 1938; and then later between 1964 and 1966, when Congress gave us the Voting Rights Act, Medicare, and the Immigration and Naturalization Act of 1965.

The pitiful voting rate in this country deserves much of the blame for this. I'm tired of hearing how several thousand white swing voters in the Detroit suburbs decided the Trump-Clinton 2016 election. Really? Let's consider the more than 100 million people who sat out that election, just as even more millions sit out the midterms. Not having voted for a lifetime, so many are now incapable of voting as a form of learned helplessness. Few if any from their families or social circles have voted, nor did they get the education that encourages or empowers them to be voters. It is fine to rail about external barriers to voting in red states, but tens of millions face psychological barriers that are just as great, which no one is trying that hard to remove or is able to remove, unless we make voting a law. At least in some cases, nonvoters lack that civic self-respect, or a sense of civic competence, having never been forced or invited to perform any civic obligation.

Toleration of their dropping out only confirms that sense of unworthiness. Many come from families where no one voted and from schools that wrote them off as lost causes as active citizens. It's hard to take a deep breath and go down a ballot if you've never done it before, especially in middle age. By then, nonvoters are so far removed from the public realm it is a waste of money to fire them up. They are the truly powerless.

Yet by virtue of this very powerlessness, they have so great a power over us. Of course they decided the election in 2016. They decide every election. Not showing up puts the gridlock in place; it capsizes the Constitution. Indeed, given the many checks and balances in our Constitution, compulsory voting is the only way to break the political gridlock that has paralyzed the country for the last fifty or so years. We need the debtor class in full force, or nearly so, to keep the creditor class in check. That's not my neo-Marxist view, it's James Madison's, in *Federalist*, No. 10. In Madison's view, without the have-not faction showing up to overcome the have faction, we end up with what we now call crony capitalism. In a sense, it is a design flaw in Madison's machinery. If the debtor class is too discouraged by the checks and balances, they stop showing up, and the checks and balances against the creditor class no longer work. Then the Gini index, which measures income inequality, goes up at the same rate as the Dow, and we end up with an even bigger plutocracy than the Federalists and their heirs in the Democratic Party elite wanted. Compulsory voting may not be necessary in other countries, but it is necessary in ours, at least given what long ago would have been the unimaginable power of our particular form of capitalism.

It is true that in the red states there are various forms of voter suppression, increasingly brazen under continued conservative rule. Still, the Constitution itself is an accidental kind of voter suppression—not by intent but by effect. In its frustration of majority rule, it undermines the norm of voting at all. Yes, I sympathize with nonvoters. I would rather throw out some of the checks and balances, which prevent UNIONISM from taking hold. I hate to quote Lincoln—it seems like a last resort—but by the end of his life, he had grasped that the divide in the country, then as it is now, comes from lack of majority rule. In his December 1864 message to the Congress, which was still dithering over the Thirteenth Amendment, he wrote, "In a great national crisis like ours, unanimity of action among those seeking a common end is very desirable—almost indispensable. And yet no such approach to unanimity is attainable unless some deference shall be paid to the will of the majority, *simply because it is the will of the majority.*" Instead, we Democrats, who should be the majority party, have long tolerated the Senate filibuster. We are as responsible for it as Mitch McConnell. And if we do not get rid of it, we will be gone in 2022 and will deserve to be gone.

Personally, I no longer care what the framers would think. By the end of his life, Lincoln knew more than they did. The House in particular has been the real injured party by the excess of checks and balances. A supermajority rule in the Senate has long been an institutional injury to the House, making it a much heavier lift for House measures to become law. As an excessive check on the House, the filibuster upends the original checks and balances, which over time, in the country we have become, are already too many. What is so galling is that the House has been so powerless to protect itself—and the people who arguably deserve the most representation are the millions of those who have completely or largely dropped out. Before and after I lost the election, I used to write as many op-eds as an uninformed freelancer is allowed to argue about why the filibuster should be destroyed. In the 1990s and even as late as 2010, I could get such pieces accepted because the argument was still a novelty. It is not that I had any foresight in 1994, when I wrote the first of them and everyone patted me on the head: it was not an insight, but a visitation, not unlike an angel appearing in a dream. In the same way, I find it hard to come up with the right reasons for compulsory voting, when I feel it like a visitation—from an angel, or from Whitman—that unless we can amend the Constitution, this is the best extraconstitutional way to majority rule.

Without compulsory voting, two bad things happen. First, we have a less representative government, or a government less capable of representing the working class. That leads to more inequality, or less mobility, and in general, less rationality— more racism, more tribalism and other forms of political bestiality. Second, and just as dangerous, with only half or more voting in presidential elections and even less than half in midterms for the Congress, we have every election decided by a rump electorate. No majority is the *real* majority when only a fraction is in and a fraction is out. Why is their rump electorate better than our rump electorate? Soon enough we have a president inciting a mob to storm the capital and state legislatures prepared to flip the outcome of elections. All of that would stop if everyone had to vote.

———————

What could be better reasons than these for compulsory voting?

In my case, one other big reason I became a convert to compulsory voting is that it is the only way to get a new working class. I am sick of the one that keeps voting GOP and tired of praying before I go to bed that things will change. Let's get a new group in here—indeed, let's try getting in the majority of the working class, or let's say the middle to the bottom in terms of income, who have never voted at all, not even once. Maybe they will be GOP voters, too. But at least they're starting without the bad habits of a lifetime.

Thomas Carlyle, the great Victorian magus, once wrote that the extension of suffrage in Disraeli's England was like "shooting Niagara." Well, I'm ready to get in a barrel and go over the falls.

After all, it would be the nuclear option in terms of ending voter suppression. Think of the changes in recent years: early voting, absentee voting, voting by mail. Now it's not just possible to vote on Sunday—which was supposed to be the cure-all—but up to three or four Sundays before Election Day in presidential and midterm elections. Can't find your polling place? It's on your phone. In comparison to forty years ago, the ballots are banging on our doors. Has it made any difference? Not really. Of course we have to block voter ID laws and other barriers in the red states. But let's assume hypothetically that we could get rid of those barriers; it's less than clear that turnout would go up. It might. Or it might not. At least one study has shown that when voting became more convenient in some places, turnout actually dropped.

Emilee Booth Chapman, an assistant professor at Stanford, does a nice job of answering various objections to compulsory voting in her essay "The Distinctive Value of Elections and the Case for Compulsory Voting." Some of them seem silly. For instance: "No, no, we just have to turn out our base." That's what I have heard all my life, and in the end it can never work. Oh, in particular cases, there will be victories, even a lot of victories, but in the long run, with civic norms so weak, the turnout of our base is a way not of ending, but of maintaining gridlock. The other side will see our victories as illegitimate—as they are, with rump electorates—and they will pull off better turnouts, too. Worse, despite all of our high-mindedness, to turn out our base requires a kind of tacit acquiescence in keeping others from not voting. To the extent that we don't want *everyone* to turn out, the Democratic Party is the party of voter suppression too.

Here's another objection for which many of you are waiting: "Maybe it is OK to fine people for not voting in Australia, but can that be justified here under the First Amendment?"

Fine. Let's talk about that.

It is not just Australia. There are other countries, such as Mexico and Guatemala, that have laws that require everyone to vote. But in many of these countries, the law is not enforced, or at least not seriously enforced. It looks like a law, but it is more of an exhortation. In Australia, it's the real thing: there is a $20 fine. Yet it's not quite as compulsory as it looks. As Professor Chapman points out, there is a ready list of legal excuses for getting out of the duty to vote, much as, when I was in college in the 1960s, there was such a list of excuses for getting out of the draft. After all, the voting rate in Australia—usually 94 percent—fell to 91 percent in 2016, and that means plenty of people are getting out. Besides, it's only a $20 fine—that's not even half of a parking ticket. You only get in trouble if you blow it off; every year, the Australian Election Commission brings thousands of suits against scofflaws.

On the other hand, even in 2016 turnout was 91 percent. It is a nuisance to do all that is required to get out of the duty to vote. One objection that Professor Chapman takes up—I have seen it elsewhere—is that with or without compulsory voting, the rate in Australia would still be 87 percent. I will spare the empirical research here, but most political scientists in Australia scoff at this claim. In the 1922 elections, before compulsory voting, the turnout in Australia had been less than 60 percent. In 1924, compulsory voting began and it has been over 90 percent ever since. Of course it makes a difference! Our own progressives should have adopted the Australian system of compulsory voting when they adopted the Australian secret ballot. Before we adopted the Australian secret ballot, the political parties in the United States used to draw up and print party ballots and pass them around for people to take to the polls and vote. Why not go all in for the Australian system? Since we have the secret ballot, why not compulsory voting too?

Anyway, the First Amendment is no bar. If compulsory voting were unconstitutional under the First Amendment, then jury duty would be even more so. If it is unconstitutional to require citizens to walk across the street and check off their names on a sheet, in secret no less, then it is vastly more unconstitutional to make them serve on a jury for what may be two weeks or two months and render an opinion as to whether someone should live or die. Of course there are certain excuses for getting out of jury duty, but that's true for voting in Australia, too.

Furthermore, a law instituting compulsory voting need not be a compulsory law to vote as such; it could be a law requiring people to vote or fill out a form to opt out. It can be a nudge. Many a behavioral economist will testify that you can design a decision format that mostly dictates the decision.

Even if there were no jury duty, and no opt-out at all, it would still be constitutional. Much of the litigation in my firm is First Amendment; I'm starting to get weary from looking up so much First Amendment law. Under the case law, I can assure you, it is often said that there must be a balancing of the burden on speech and the government interest. In this case, there would be no burden on expression at all, since anyone could cast a blank ballot and even that would remain a secret; and on the other hand, the government can serve an important regulatory interest, namely promoting the values of citizenship and inclusion and ensuring the legitimacy of our elected government.[1]

———————————

But let's put aside the First Amendment. Maybe it's a question of conscience. Many people—even if it is a tiny fraction of the electorate—think abstaining from the vote is an important symbolic act. But come now: can it be so symbolic or expressive if no one sees you doing it? In the civic realm, your *cri de coeur* is like the proverbial tree falling in the forest with no one around.

OK, the system is rigged. We're so impressed that you've figured it out. Why don't you inspire the rest of us by not paying a fine?

Let's get real. Look at who the nonvoters really are, according to the Pew Foundation study of the 100 million-plus Americans who sat out the Trump-Clinton election. It was nothing personal; most sit out every election. Disproportionately, the Pew Foundation study found, nonvoters are the young, voters of Hispanic descent, and people who are deep in debt. Yes, some used to vote and have

1 To be sure, some will mock me for saying that the Supreme Court will follow precedent. I am not saying it will, just that this is the case law. Go ahead. Look it up. It's in the much-cited *Burdick v. Takushi* (1992), the gist of which is a quote from *Anderson v. Celebrezze* (1983). It's the law that conservative and not liberal justices developed.

now stopped, saying that voting doesn't matter. But even most of this latter set of nonvoters come from backgrounds where voting was not a norm. And most nonvoters have never voted at all. Ever. Or had parents who ever voted. That's why we should see it as a kind of learned helplessness: learned from parents at home, learned from peers, learned from others with the same learned helplessness. Nonvoting is part of the larger inequality that only *voting itself* can end. In that sense, compulsory voting is a form of reparation for denial of their right to an equal, high-quality education that would have equipped them to make a real choice about whether to vote or not. In Melville's famous description of existential paralysis, his hero Bartleby says, "I would prefer not to." But most nonvoters do not "choose." They are not like Bartleby sending a message, even in code. It is a status inflicted on them—a kind of low-status civic servitude or bondage from which compulsory voting could free them. Sometimes, a bit of compulsion does make us free, just as Title VII of the Civil Rights Act freed many whites whom the culture forced into demeaning Black persons, or freed men from demeaning women. Or think about the Australians. Because they are compelled to vote, they may paradoxically have less need of it, because now they have the norm or the habit of voting. If we require the 100 million (or far more in midterm years) to start being citizens in at least this minimal sense, our own people may embrace the norm of voting too.

––––––––––

Let's get to the biggest objection: it's *impossible*. "You might just as well ask for labor law reform, because it's just as unlikely

Congress will do this." That's true: we can forget Congress. Even at the national level, all at once, in every state, it would be unthinkable that Congress would do it.

No, it would have to come from the states. Let me explain how it might happen.

Thanks to Article I, section 2 of the Constitution, the states set the rules for suffrage. Forget the federal level. We can enact compulsory voting in individual states—at least the blue ones to start. It is true enough that Congress would have the power to stop such a state law, at least in federal elections. That's a worry. But let's assume Congress is too dysfunctional to stop a state that chose to do it. Besides, it is hard to see how Congress could stop states from having compulsory voting in their own state elections, which are usually concurrent with the federal ones.

It may be that if only one or two blue states put it in, it will change very little. But it is more likely that it would change everything, though perhaps not at first and not all at once. For one thing, it would seem that, eventually, it would lead to the end of the Electoral College. It could also lead to the end of flipping the control of the Congress in midterm elections, when often just a bit more than a third of the electorate participates. It also might reduce the dark money and corporate money that is currently so important in turning out the vote.

Let's go through what might happen:

Suppose one state, like California, perhaps by referendum, adopted compulsory voting. That in itself could go a long way to bringing about the end of the Electoral College, a nasty piece of business which has installed two losers, Bush and Trump, as president in this still young century, and may yet install even more. Suppose California had compulsory voting in 2016. And now imagine 95 percent turnout in the state with the same split of Clinton and Trump votes. Then, instead of *three* million votes nationally, Hillary Clinton would have won the popular vote by around *seven* million votes nationally, just based on the difference in California's results. (Pardon me for using round numbers.) Now suppose New York—inspired by all of this—did the same. Then Illinois followed. Then Massachusetts did it. Assuming no change in the split, Hillary Clinton could easily have won by *fifteen* million votes nationally. Even in the United States, it would be too much. It would throw the country into turmoil. The red states, where states' rights are defended ad nauseum on talk radio and TV screens, would be furious. We would have two competing forms of government and only one could survive. As Lincoln once said—and I promise to stop quoting him—"a house divided against itself cannot stand." Or as the economist Herbert Stein once said, formulating Stein's law: "If something cannot go on forever, it will stop."

So which of these two competing forms of government would survive?

The smart money would be on the UNION to win. Once we "extend" the suffrage in so many states, it would be impossible to take it back.

———

Compulsory voting would also lead to the end of another kind of minority rule: the way a third of the electorate can flip the control of the House and the Senate in a midterm election year. This would go a long way toward stabilizing the government. It is shameful that right now, as I write, we high-five each other over the turnout in the midterm election of 2018. It was still a rump electorate, even if it was larger than the norm.

Last of all, it might—I hope—bring down the cost of elections, in which billions are spent simply to turn out the base. Here comes everyone: the law now does the mobilizing. And even if some white nationalists come out of hiding to vote, we will be better off. Here's why.

Nonvoters are young. Why not get them in the habit of voting while the sap is still rising and they are falling into each other's arms? We are more likely to get a government of the future. It would be terrible for them to cast their first vote much later, when they are old and dried up and just want to settle scores.

Nonvoters are deep in debt. Or poor. A welfare state will be impossible until we get all the beneficiaries of it to vote.

Nonvoters are disproportionately Latino, perhaps the likeliest of any voting bloc to support UNIONISM over Trump-type nationalism.

Some polls suggest that nonvoters are moderates, and if these moderates vote en masse, an ever-shriller GOP will pay the price. If we just get free of gridlock, the country will drift left, albeit more slowly than one might like. Even in the worst case for the Left, it will still have a glacial effect that will end the Right's hothead form of minority rule.

For a moment, though, let me stop being high-minded about citizenship and inclusion and just say it outright—compulsory voting will help the Democrats, even if more white nationalists end up voting, too. Even those on the left who are hostile to compulsory voting should give it that much.

If in place, compulsory voting will make a wealth tax easier. It will make labor law reform easier. It will make a hike in Social Security easier. Best of all, it will force the Democrats to have a bigger working-class base or to stop thinking they can get away without having one. Yes, compulsory voting will be a crisis for the party, and I say bring it on. At the next convention, give the delegates copies of "Crossing Brooklyn Ferry" and resolve to get the whole country on board.

Might they be "low information" voters? That was the old sexist argument against giving women the right to vote. But when American women did get the right to vote in 1919, many became better informed—maybe better informed than the men. By 1924, the League of Women Voters was organized in 346 of the then 433 congressional districts.

Oh, I know what you're thinking: Steve Bannon is out there in his lair, like a minotaur, just waiting for these new voters to stumble along. "Come on in, my pretties." Isn't *Breitbart* a risk?

Of course it's a risk. I said we were shooting Niagara. We don't trust the poorly educated. But surely nonvoters must have built up some immunity to Fox News or else they would be watching it now and voting for Trump. They are, by definition, contagion-free. And we can take heart from the massive original research set out in *Network Propaganda: Manipulation, Disinformation, and Radicalization in American Politics* (2018). The three authors—Yochai Benkler, Robert Faris, and Hal Roberts—calculate that more than two-thirds of the country are just outside the closed-loop, far right media world of Fox News and Steve Bannon. That is, they live in a world where there are some standards of objectivity. It's likely that at least two-thirds of nonvoters, and maybe more, would have a connection to the bigger, fact-grounded world. Besides, right-wing media offers an intense political fantasy life for people who feel they are disenfranchised—it's the tinker mentality that inspired John Bunyan's *The Pilgrim's Progress*—while nonvoters typically do not care about the franchise and are not looking for political fantasy lives at all.

I must be done with the objections. But no, here's another: "You say compulsory voting is great, but there's all sorts of fighting in Australia. I read where they're now fighting immigration."

OK, look, even with compulsory voting, political sin will continue. Not even compulsory voting takes away that freedom. For instance, in their 2018 and 2019 elections, the country followed the global rightward trend in selecting a center-right/right-wing coalition government over the Labor opposition. But Australia and Belgium, where voting is also enforced, are still better than us at being social democracies, and they are more egalitarian, in fact. Indeed, if there had been compulsory voting in Germany and other countries, it might have kept the European Social Democrat Left in power. Had the voting rate been not just 75 percent, but 91 percent or higher, the Social Democratic Left might have been in office in most of the last twenty to thirty years. It's been out of office because the voter turnout rate in even egalitarian countries has relatively declined. It's compulsory voting that would put the Left in power, give it the few extra points it needs.

Any final objection? Yes: *it's so utopian.*

Well, California is a utopian place, and it's far from utopian to imagine it in place there, and once in place, then it's in play.

The real objection, of course, is that, deep down, we liberals don't believe that we the people can be trusted to govern ourselves.

Here's my closing argument for compulsory voting: it is there to stop despair. Had we kept just those in despair from dropping out of politics, it might have kept us safe from Trump. There is a line that runs through Orwell's *1984*, which a better writer would find too corny to quote. Should I quote it? Probably not, but I will. It's what the novel's hero, Winston Smith, keeps saying: "If there is hope, it lies in the proles."

The working class sitting it out in *1984* is like the nonvoter working class that is sitting it out now. Hope for the Democratic Party lies in those who currently sit our elections out—out of political and psychological isolation, out of exhaustion, out of generations-long habit. Well, of course, even in this chapter I end up arguing for what, deep down, is one more version of labor law reform.

But maybe it is not the working class but the young who will have to save us.

CHAPTER FIVE:

WHY BERNIE AND I ARE NOT REALLY SOCIALISTS

After losing the election—I know, I keep saying this—I ran into a state politician. She came up and frowned: "I hear you ran as a socialist." Aghast, I started to deny it, and then I saw she was laughing.

OK, very funny.

Well, that was 2009. After the Sanders campaign years later, no one would have teased me. Maybe like him, I should have run as a socialist. Or, like Sanders, I should have at least pitched to the young—not the defeated working class west of I-90/I-94. Yes, I had my three issues: Social Security, single-payer healthcare, and railing at the bank bailout; issues that I thought might flip at least a few of the people I represent as a labor lawyer. But who am I kidding? Maybe the decency of a Biden will bring back a few, except there was never any "back" for them to go back to. I know I should have expected the vote for Trump in 2016 and even in 2020—the working class had been voting GOP for years. But this time it was unforgiveable. They were voting for someone who said, even in 2016, he would not accept the outcome unless he won. The good thing about working-class support for Trump—it helped to keep me jogging, so I could work out my fury at having wasted my life. I used to argue with myself:

"I poured out my life for them!"

"Fine—but they didn't ask you to do that."

"Except when they're in my office."

"You're criticizing them—it's so elitist."

"And not criticizing them—it's even more elitist."

Well, I have stopped arguing with myself. Everyone looks back on a wasted life. But I was a fool to think I could get votes west of the Kennedy.

If I could do it over, I would pitch to the young working class, who are not ruined yet. The young and the old—that is a bigger divide now, I think, than it was when I was young in the 1960s.

So why didn't I try?

Because the young told me not to try. Julie, our campaign manager, our field director, every volunteer I had, were all in their twenties. They scoffed at the idea: "Don't bother—you can't get them to vote."

I'm for compulsory voting if only to speed up the young taking over the country. It is our duty to turn it over to them—now, right now, before they marry, have children, and start driving SUVs. Make them begin to govern and then see what they do when we get out of their way.

The young face an existential threat—climate change— greater than people my age ever did. For our generation, in the US and Europe, the threat was the Bomb going off. But it was never all that likely, and there was always New Zealand. Eventually, the USSR collapsed, which came as a surprise to me, as I thought it had collapsed previously. But while our existential threat petered out, a much bigger and hotter Armageddon is coming at the next generation full blast, and there is no place, not even New Zealand, where it is possible to escape it.

They have every right to be for socialism, if it is necessary to keep the earth inhabitable, to replace the capitalism that will kill them. For that reason, while "generations" are usually not the same as social or economic classes, the young may be such a class—a class of those who are about to bake, if not die, in temperatures that reach 130 degrees Fahrenheit. It's right out there, in the science, and every year the estimates are worse.

There is no point in representative government—for them—unless it is a debate about how to overhaul the form of capitalism that is threatening to kill us—or even what form of socialism might replace it.

Otherwise, it does not matter whether we abolish the Senate or pump up the People's House.

Because I am a labor lawyer, some may suppose I am a socialist like Sanders. It's true—trade unions are the most socialist thing that socialists ever invented. But neither Sanders nor I are socialists, at least in espousing the real thing—at least in the original nineteenth-century sense, with the abolition of private property or the end of wage labor. Single-payer healthcare and free college are both things that President Harry Truman once proposed. Such watered-down social democracy is not even close to real socialism. I have already mentioned *Capitalism, Alone: The Future of the System That Rules the World*, by Branko Milanović. Here's what it is: wage labor, for private profit, for the benefit of a relative few who are the owners of real property and financial wealth. He identifies three states of this system: the industrial capitalism of the early twentieth century, the social democratic capitalism that went from the New Deal to the 1970s, and now what he calls the "liberal meritocratic" capitalism of our own time, highly unequal and becoming more so. It takes its most extreme form in the US; in China, and some of Southeast Asia, it is instead a capitalism run by the state or a political class, not quite as corrupt as Russia but getting there (it turns out that communism was not an alternative to capitalism but a transition to a form of it).

But why isn't it possible to have something radically different?

I am too old to be a socialist, and yet I'm still a believer in just social democracy. But if I were in my twenties, I would have a life-or-death determination for socialism to be an alternative. If it is not up for debate, I fear there is no reason for the young—I mean *all* of the young, not just the elite—to vote or to even take up citizenship as a way of life. I'm stuck in my own New Deal world. It's unfair to expect the young to figure it out. But that's what they should do.

Of course, people my age haven't exactly left them in a good position to figure it out. They already have been as corrupted by capitalism as much as my friends or me. Thanks to us, the world is too much with us, as the poet Wordsworth complained. It's impossible for the standard of living to stop going up, even if it kills us. There is just too much *stuff*. During the pandemic, the lobby of my condo building piled up every day with gifts conferred on us by drivers from Amazon and UPS. The world was too much with us, even when it was with us less. It seems impossible for anyone, old or young, to break free from the freedom to consume.

But when the temperature hits not just 100 degrees Fahrenheit but 130 or higher, we will have to "go big," in the phrase of the day—as in REALLY big—in a much bigger way than a $15 minimum wage. As a species, we will have to adapt at a speed unknown to prior versions of *homo sapiens*. So what would it look like—real socialism, now? It would need to be a specific utopia, not a dreamy dream, which was our great grandfather's version of socialism, and which, in any case, is now a corpse. Whatever it is, it cannot be state socialism. It was the state socialist USSR that, with Chernobyl, inflicted the single biggest one-off environmental wound on the planet.

So, what are the details of this new model utopia? Well, whatever it is, it first has to eliminate or radically curb the elements of capitalism: wage labor, private property, and production based on profit for a few entrepreneurs. Beyond that . . .

It is a commonplace to say that Marx had no good idea of it, that the old socialism was weak on the specific design of what would replace capitalism. The lack of a good working utopia is probably the biggest thing that now holds back a worldwide socialist movement. Otherwise, all the elements are in place. In Donald Sassoon's *One Hundred Years of Socialism*—which I should say is mostly European socialism, which is above all German socialism—he says there needs be three core beliefs, namely:

Capitalism is unfair. Even at Goldman Sachs they think so. In Milanović's view, the unfairness of liberal meritocratic capitalism, at least in its extreme US form, is most acute in education and financial wealth. I already took up his point about public education, which is far less democratic now. As to financial wealth, the elite not only have far too much of it, but they also now hog the higher salary income. At least in the nineteenth century, when Thorstein Veblen was writing *The Theory of the Leisure Class* and Trollope was writing novels, people at the top would have been horrified at living the 24-7 life of CEOs now: it would be a huge reduction in the unfairness of capitalism if we could go back to the time when the elite worked much less. But in my own case, I really have done nothing or very little to get a fabulous increase in my financial wealth just because—turned down by several young women for marriage many years ago—I miserably put away what I once thought was a modest amount of money in a 401(k). By mishandling my romantic life, I came by accident to find out why the inequality in wealth is so wholly undeserved. It should have made a socialist.

Capitalism is obsolete. It is now, even if it was not back then. We have come a long way since the time of *The Communist Manifesto.* As John Maynard Keynes was arguing almost a hundred years ago, the economic problem—the core problem of the human race—should be on the verge of being solved in our own century. While distribution is a big problem, we have enough stuff. Capitalism is a terrible system for the fair distribution of what is already much too much. And that's the least of why it is obsolete. Marx used to write about capitalism's internal contradictions. So much "surplus" value would have been taken out of wage labor that there would not be enough people who were able to consume. It turned out that, as Keynes helped to show, the government can do the consuming. Or better, it can pay you and me to consume. Go ahead, eat it up. Solving *that* internal contradiction was a piece of cake. As it turns out, there is a much bigger internal contradiction. It's not in our consuming all that production, but in nature gagging on it. We're using up all that capital, which Marx never included in *Das Kapital.* To him it was taken for granted: he used to write about "culture" rising up against "nature," in that vague Teutonic way that was his style. He never thought about "nature" rising up against "culture," as we are experiencing now. We are running out of air and water for capitalist production. Furthermore, private ownership makes less sense when the thing produced is knowledge or an idea. It may work for agrarian capitalism for someone to own the land. It may be true for industrial capitalism for someone to own the machines that make the widgets. But capitalism is an awkward structure in an economy that is producing knowledge or distributing ideas. Maybe there is a better way than private ownership by the very rich over knowledge and ideas. But let's turn for now to the third core belief.

There is a homogenous working class. In one sense, this seems untrue: this book has made a big point about the divide, and even why college-educated people have an incentive to accentuate the difference between themselves and the high school grads they supervise. It is to get a return on all that human capital that they and their parents spent so much money to install in them. On the other hand, the burning of the planet is bad for everyone, and those workers of the world with higher incomes have arguably more to lose. In some ways, the exploitation of the more educated has its own special cruelty, for in their long schooling, they have been educated for the consumption of leisure and a form of culture from which—because they work so much—they are being deprived. Though there may not be a homogeneous working class, there is more reason than ever for workers to unite.

So how do they get to utopia? Well, I have three ideas:

Bring back pension fund socialism. We should collectivize wealth. That sounds like the USSR, but it's taking a New Deal invention and pushing it much farther. In 1974, as I was getting out of law school, there appeared a curious book—*The Unseen Revolution: How Pension Fund Socialism Came to America* by Peter Drucker. At that time, so-called defined benefit pension plans, which have now disappeared in most of the private sector, covered three-fifths of American workers. Today it is well under a fifth. But at that time, as Drucker argued, working people were on their way to *owning* America. The pension and welfare funds constituted 25 percent of the capital wealth of the country. That "unseen revolution," in slow motion even then, was about to stop, but if we brought back a labor movement that covered everyone, that collectivization of wealth could start up again. This time, we might do it in the original version, before the Taft-Hartley Act of 1947 changed the rules, when workers themselves, through union-appointed trustees, had complete control over the investments. Senator Taft and Congressman Hartley, over Harry Truman's veto, had enough clout to bar the workers from running it; otherwise, we might already have had the socialism. But it is conceptually possible to kickstart the same collectivization of wealth that was going on at that time. If we got to 25 percent, we could start over and aim not for a quarter, but for half or more.

I say worker-owned, but you and I as workers would not save our money individually like in a 401(k) or an IRA—or individually own it at all. The only way hourly workers ever save money is when they save it collectively, as a group, by a group decision that overrides what we might do with it individually. The only way working people ever save is by compulsion—it's taken out of their hands. That's what is wrong with reparations or redistribution to people through taxes. Eventually, those individual payments are recycled into the bank accounts of the rich.

The only way to share the wealth is to collectivize it, to keep it safe not just from predators, but from ourselves, acting on our own worst instincts. I am so sorry I missed out on pension fund socialism. Protecting those pools of worker-owned capital would have been my career.

To the working-class young, I can only say: jump on this right away. And then capitalism, as the state is supposed to do under socialism, will start to wither away. Now to the second idea.

Almost eliminate private property. Well, I do not want to eliminate private property. It helps people build character. Not *all* property is theft. But it should be treated more like we treat the shoreline of Lake Michigan. Owners should be more like trustees. I have been waiting for pages here to get to the story of our firm's case against George Lucas. It was a suit to stop him from erecting a Star Wars museum on the banks of Lake Michigan—in the most breathtaking spot on the front yard of the Loop. As we claimed in the suit, this was land held in public trust, recovered from the ancient lake bed of a much bigger Lake Michigan. Under law that went back to King Ethelred, or his equivalent, such land recovered from the sea cannot be sold or given away. The land in this case was not government property. It could not be "owned" by the state of Illinois or the city of Chicago, which had no power to sell or dispose of it. It was held in a trust for all the people of the state, and the state or the city had the limited power only to act as trustees.

Well, I must say, property law professors love to write about a form of property so out of the capitalism box and yet so ancient; no one can get at it, at least in theory. I should not exaggerate. We did not "win" the case in any normal sense, but we created a legal tangle that might have taken years to resolve. Lucas took his museum to LA, where such a museum is much happier.

So, if the planet is burning, why not hold all property in public trust or a limited form of it? We have to stop the drawing down of nature as a form of free capital. There would still be individual ownership, but like the city and the state in the case of Lake Michigan shoreline, those owners would also be trustees. They would have greater legal obligations to the public for how they dispose of the land, and they would be under a strict duty as trustees not to engage in any form of profit taking without a strict accounting to the public. We need not figure out all the trust obligations all at once; we can figure it out case by case, as we have figured out the law of trusts over the last ten centuries. The point is to put the obligations in place now, so that those who scoff at these new obligations will proceed in the future at their own legal risk.

It may seem too far out to go too far back in time. But this new kind of ownership, in this time of Armageddon, would have a passing resemblance to medieval or feudal tenure. In *The Ancient Law* (1861), the great legal scholar Henry Maine described the progress of civilization as a change from "status" to "contract." But perhaps to save civilization, we have to revert. In the socialist utopia, owners would also have a "status," as trustees for nonowners, especially with respect to the use of air and water and natural resources. It's also an affirmative duty to take care of nonowners, and here I borrow the argument of Joseph Singer, a Harvard property law professor, in *The Edges of the Field*. The title refers to a command in the Book of Leviticus that a property owner has a duty to leave to the poor and the stranger the gleanings of the crop "at the edge of the field."

The Book of Leviticus will only take us so far. We need one more thing as well:

Build like Red Vienna. In October 2019, right before the pandemic, I went to the city that was once called "Red Vienna." Over champagne with a professor, I found out about an exhibit, "Red Vienna, 1918–1931," that was on display at City Hall. As the exhibit makes clear, "Red Vienna" at this time was an attempt at a new kind of socialism, summed up in this poster I saw:

No—to Social Democracy

No—to Bolshevik Communism

Yes—to Continuing Education

And like the ruins of a Mayan civilization, Red Vienna itself is gone, but a good chunk of it is still there, out on the street. Right now, in Karl Marx Hof, and housing like it, the low- and middle-income people are still living together just as Red Vienna imagined it. It's true, the units are small, but the whole place is hip and much desired. No one has to pay more than 20 or 25 percent of their income for rent. As the young stay on and their income goes up, they still pay no more in rent. Over a quarter of the citizens rent directly from the City of Vienna. Another half or so rent from not-for-profit owners.

This is the housing in which we all should be living to lower our rich-world carbon footprint. It is a shelter from the ecological brimstone to come. It's where we can pick up the virtuous habit of looking out for each other. But now that we have the building plan for continuing education, what might be the continuing education that would go on inside?

Well, let's think of something that is different from social democratic capitalism and from Bolshevik Communism— something that would be a "no" to both. Whatever "continuing education" might have meant to the artist who made the poster, I think it is something different, perhaps "lifetime" skill-based education, such as it now exists in Denmark. It is more than just going back in midlife and picking up a new skill, even if it is a more ubiquitous twenty-first-century skill. Nor can it be education by the state, even if in some form the state can require it. For this continuing education to be different from social democracy or state socialism, an element of it has to be time off, with pay—in effect, a year's worth of a universal basic income at some point between the age of thirty and sixty-two. It should be for introspection and service to others. Everyone should be forced to travel at some point in it, and the farther from the United States, the better. At least in this country, and in the rest of the rich developed world, we have the money to do it without penalizing us for any lost Social Security and pension credit thanks to a year away from work. Just let people go. Maybe there should be a requirement to offer counseling at a local high school, community college, or four-year college. Whatever it is, continuing education in the rich world has to be a self-education in doing something other than working, and letting older people exercise the right to be young.

Whatever the future of socialism may be, it has to be true to the vision John Maynard Keynes laid out in his 1930 essay "Economic Possibilities for Our Grandchildren." About the time Red Vienna was collapsing, Keynes calculated that in about a hundred years—let's say, 2021—the economic problem would be solved.

A recent biography of Keynes by Zachary Carter elaborates why Keynes came to this conclusion. Most of us are not adding all that much to our standard of living; what we do for our "work" is just an excuse for someone to pay us money so we can continue to consume. Of course, there would have to be some work—but far less than we are now doing. As Keynes wrote, it is hard to get rid of the old Adam, and now the same thing has also gotten into Eve. But for all I add to the general standard of living as a lawyer, I might just as well stop. It may be true for you as well. Let the state just pay me and you and the rest of us who are not really needed in the workforce so we can go on consuming.

Of course, continuing education assumes a fair distribution of income and wealth, and we're far from that. But Keynes's point is that it need not be pure communism for human flourishing to start. Even more than in 1930, we need a form of continuing education to connect us to the natural world, even in a religious sense, and to disconnect us from technology. We need to be able to go out for a while but always to come back.

Anyway, it's up to the young to figure out what continuing education would be. Personally, I would assign some poetry. How can that hurt? Congress is no more likely to enact any of this than it would be to move the nation's capital to São Paulo. It's time to get back to why I was running for the House.

CHAPTER SIX:
ABOLISH THE SENATE

Had I somehow snuck into the House, I might have made a career of trying to abolish the Senate. It is the only way the House can be the People's House. It is the only way for Congress to have the capacity to act, and to keep the court and the executive branch from taking over the lawmaking function. But it is also to remove the check that Idaho and North Dakota have over our lives.

As a form of representation, the Senate must go, and with it the filibuster. For it is not even constitutional. While not outright prohibited, Article I only notes a few specific instances in which the Senate can use a supermajority, such as to ratify treaties. If there is any other use, it should at least be by law, passed by both chambers, for a supermajority in one chamber, like the Senate, is a huge extraconstitutional blow to the ability of the other chamber to do the people's will.

Note: I revere Barack Obama. He is getting too much blame for failing to ditch the filibuster; had he tried, the rest of his party would have refused to go along. But he does bear the blame for saying he would change the way that Washington does business without any intent of taking on the filibuster. But the Senate has been an evil long before the filibuster came along. And it will be even if the filibuster goes away.

The Senate held back the first New Deal from what FDR intended, and it will hold back the second which we now deserve. Even if Trump is gone, we are still at a moment like the one the country faced in 1932—there is not just the fear and uncertainty and the sense of being unmoored, but also the doubt that our form of government is capable of coping with it all. In a way it is even worse. Unlike 1932, a real-life plot against America is already in full swing. We as a people are more uncertain than ever as to who we even are. It may be worse when the 2022 midterms are upon us and the tiny majority we have in the Senate and a gerrymandered House are gone. Right now, we're in the easy part: spending trillions to recover from the pandemic and maybe partly dialing back the tax cuts of the Trump Era. The much harder part, the real emergency, the global climate challenge, is just a few years ahead.

The problem is the Constitution itself, which still privileges that part of the country that first held back, and then wrecked, the original New Deal. Thanks to the Senate, our form of government still overrepresents the racist and populist parts of the country, the parts that most engage in magical thinking. It also now overrepresents those parts that are the biggest losers in the global economy—and by no coincidence, it made easier the rise of Trump. Even if Republican senators from these states by and large are more genteel than the Republican members of the US House, they are the real screamers, the ones who give voice to the country's id, or rather the parts that are most raw and red and racist.

That's why the Senate, for all its good manners and gentility, is a greater threat to our freedom as a people than the raucous and badly behaved House, at least when it has a GOP majority. If North Dakota has the same power as New York to determine the will of the country as a whole, it makes it impossible to act on behalf of the people as a whole—the people that we really are. And it makes it impossible for the country to be free, as a country is free only to the extent that the country is subject to the will of the people as a whole. And if the country is not free, we as a people are not free as individuals. We are right to be fearful.

Disoriented enough by all that's happening around us, we are disoriented all the more because we try to see ourselves in the strange fun house mirror of the "United States" as it is reflected in the Senate and, in effect, in the entire federal government. It is not just that the Senate represents a distorted version of the United States, but it also deprives us of knowing who we really are. Not knowing who we are, we doubt our capacity to act. We grow up not believing in our ability to govern ourselves.

That is especially true of the young, including the activist young who were bitter about the defeat of Bernie Sanders. But let's suppose Sanders had won and neither Raphael Warnock nor Jon Ossoff had taken Senate seats in Georgia. The Sanders presidency would have been as futile as Obama's, and that's far more likely to be true than it would be under a Biden presidency. The young would have turned away from Sanders and felt betrayed, and rightly so. Like the other Democrats who ran in the primaries, he had failed to explain that without the Senate, his presidency would be meaningless. Or that it would be meaningless except to the extent that by executive order or Supreme Court appointment, he could flip the finger at Mitch McConnell.

Neither Sanders nor any other Democratic candidate will go to Madison Square Garden and stand there and tell the truth: "Unless you also put in place a Senate that represents who we are as a people, which won't happen until we change the Constitution, I can't promise to deliver on anything at all." The GOP presidential nominees can always deliver on their promises: the Senate is set up to suit what little use they make of it and otherwise keep the Democrats, when they're in the White House, from governing at all. But Democratic presidential nominees, all of them, even the best, have to mislead, if not lie. So deceit becomes part of the culture and even the language. In our political culture, we have to find ways of talking around the Senate. It's an "as if" language—as if there were a representative form of government, based on one person, one vote. As Foucault might point out, we have a discourse of representation that has to ignore the Constitution, which does not permit certain things to be said.

A good example is the filibuster. We have learned to say that such and such a bill was defeated in the Senate, when a majority of the Senate had voted to pass it. We have learned to talk about a vote that was fifty-five to forty-five in favor, "as if" it were fifty-five to forty-five against. But to speak truthfully is too hard, and in a sense, too painful. So lying even to ourselves about our real form of government becomes a habit we all have. I know that I go through long stretches of lying to myself too. Both Sanders and Biden owe their years in power to the systematic denial of the principle of one person, one vote. Neither can even conceive of the existence of the Senate as a problem, much less the fundamental problem. And this leads to a general failure to think of freedom in the right way—for we think of freedom primarily as freedom from the state. But as I noted above, there is a different view of freedom—one that recognizes that our freedom as individuals depends on the state being free.

In *Liberty before Liberalism* (1998) the historian Quentin Skinner described an earlier idea of liberty, or idea of freedom, which came partly from Machiavelli and writers like John

Milton and others, now more obscure, who wrote at the time of the English Civil War. Skinner wished to distinguish our modern sense of liberty, as an individual freedom *from* the state, from their view of liberty, which depended on the freedom *of* the state to act on behalf of *the entire people,* as we really are: "If a state or commonwealth is to be counted as free, the laws that govern it must be enacted with the consent of all its citizens, the members of the body politic as a whole." It must be the will of *that* people, the actual people, and not a *faux* version of the people, or a fun house mirror of the people. "To the extent this does not happen, the body politic will be moved to act by a will other than its own," Skinner added. And if the body politic is deprived of liberty, the rest of us have no individual liberty.

The young grow up in a country that's a dysfunctional family, where no one is saying out loud what is wrong. No one, no president or presidential nominee—not Obama, not Biden, and not Sanders, had he become one—is willing to speak against the Constitution. Eventually, of course, the young—who now march for a Green New Deal or march against racism—will marry and move into middle age, and one day, grudgingly, half consciously, they'll move at least a little to the right or maybe a lot. But many will never entirely lose that particular sense that the young often have that somebody is lying about something, that in this land of the free, there is something terribly wrong

The first step, as in any dysfunctional family, or country, is to start telling the truth. And the truth is that the Constitution does not represent us, and we the people are subject to a will other than our own. It is to stop elevating the president as an omnipotent agent of change—which both the Right and Left do—because even in the glory years of Franklin Roosevelt, the Congress is far more important, unless there is rule by decree. As Ira Katznelson argues in *Fear Itself: The New Deal and the Origins of Our Time* (2014), the New Deal was nothing more than what horrifically racist senators from the South were willing to permit—or at least forbear from stopping. The New Deal existed on the condition that many of its landmark laws would not apply in the South, usually by exempting agriculture. That's how we lost organized labor in this country. The New Deal was based on a deal with the Senate that the labor movement stay locked up in the North. Years later, as the US economy moved to the union-free South and West, we stopped having much of a labor movement at all.

Yes, the Senate's departure from the principle of one person, one vote is mindboggling. In the case of the filibuster, forty senators from states representing 6 percent of the population are capable in a mathematical sense of blocking a bill. Perhaps a better measure of our lack of liberty, senators from states representing 16 percent of the people are enough to enact a bill—that is, assuming there is no filibuster. And like the Senate in the New Deal, this Senate of our day overrepresents the worst parts of the country—albeit in the most genteel way—in a way that creates a sense that we are out of control in our own country. Let's put aside the percentages set out above or even the hope that demography will flip Texas or Florida into blue states. Look at the map of the country. Compared to the coasts, the vast interior of the country can seem relatively empty. I know in my own state—in downstate Illinois—there is no one there. If it were not for the cars, it would be easy to think it is still the 1940s. And of course people are leaving, or not moving, as the rest of the country grows. To be sure, the state of Illinois is far from the worst example because it has Chicago, our biggest city of the interior and the only major American city that is not hugging up against an ocean as if it were scared to go too far inland. Our vast underpopulated interior, like the old South, becomes a bigger player in the Senate as it loses its relative importance in the country. There is every reason to think that in the next thirty years, the country will be more ungovernable than ever—and the country will have even less freedom or liberty to act.

It is the Senate which has kept in place throughout our history an especially reckless form of capitalism, in which a relative few of us, like Tom and Daisy in *The Great Gatsby*, can smash up the economy and drive on. The Senate was their legal guardian long before anyone had heard of Mitch McConnell. In our first fourscore and seven years, the Senate had the effect of overrepresenting the slave states, and locking in slavery, until the South made the colossal error of firing on Fort Sumter and starting the Civil War. Then, in the Gilded Age, thanks to the corrupt state legislatures that "elected" senators, and the railroads that bought them, the Senate had the effect of locking in our current form of capitalism. This was the real era of dark money. Of course, in the South, the Senate locked in Jim Crow and a new form of slavery and a racist authoritarian government. Then the Senate blocked and then slowly rolled back the much more egalitarian New Deal; and then, in our own time, on at least three occasions since 1976, a Senate filibuster blocked labor law reform, a true right to unionize, that had been passed by the House. And so we have the inequality of the Gilded Age. The function of the Senate, from 1787 on, has been to threaten free labor. And thanks to the filibuster, it has not mattered that the Democrats from time to time get a simple majority in the Senate. At the start of the Obama administration, there was high hope for labor law reform. At the AFL-CIO, people high-fived each other. "We have sixty votes"; that is, enough to beat a filibuster. But sixty votes are never sixty votes in the Senate, because the Senate, or at least one senator, is always for sale, and it is an illusion to think that so long as the filibuster exists, sixty votes can ever lead to an end of our Gilded Age or put a stop to the burning of the planet.

Of the two great arguments in favor of the Senate, the first is that it increases bipartisanship. Yet the Senate, especially in recent times, has destroyed bipartisanship. Far from empowering moderates, it has led to a purge of them, especially in the GOP. It is the logical consequence of a form of government so far from majority rule. Thanks to the Senate, the minority party like the GOP can shut down the majority party for years. It can do so without trying to be the majority party, and that means it does not have to be a responsible opposition party. It does not have to worry whether or not it is perceived to be bipartisan.

And in fact, because of the Senate's cockeyed representation of the country, it can be a minority party nationally but a majority one in the Senate. It also tears apart the Democrats who are the majority party, or at least the party that wishes to make use of the government. For if the GOP can get away with doing nothing, the Democrats have no alternative except to do something. So the Democratic Party is always being split in two, or appears to be split in two, between the side that wants a deal and the side that wants purity of heart. That in turn makes it harder for the Democrats to unify as a party, as they could if the only chamber of Congress happened to be the People's House. There is no one like Joe Manchin in the lower house.

The other argument for the Senate is original intent, as equal suffrage of the states in the Senate was the price for having a United States at all. That's why we have a nation— the Grand Compromise of 1787, the New Jersey Plan and not the Virginia Plan. We have to accept the Senate as the rules of the game, which now take three-quarters of the states to change and so the rules will never change. Indeed, the Constitution itself says that every amendment is possible except an amendment to abolish the equal suffrage of the states in the Senate. Did you know that? Of course, you could amend the Constitution to get rid of that provision and then go on to amend the Senate. But the argument is: a rejection of the Senate is a rejection of the Constitution.

Let's put aside the fact that Madison, Hamilton, and the other real geniuses of the Constitution hated the idea of equal suffrage in the Senate and that Madison in particular was emphatic about opposing it. Let's also forget that the framers who thought otherwise tended to be the worst of them, the slaveholders of South Carolina and Georgia. For that matter, let's forget the Constitution itself is an illegal act. From the Continental Congress, the delegates to the convention had only the narrower mandate of amending the Articles of Confederation and the amending of the Articles took a unanimous vote. Instead, the framers went rogue, drafting a whole Constitution to be adopted for thirteen states if just nine agreed. The Constitution is an illegal compact, which should be without effect by any standard that would hold up in a court. It's legal or legitimate only in the sense that Lawrence Lessig described in a recent book, *Fidelity and*

Constraint: How the Supreme Court Has Read the American Constitution. It was legal or legitimate, Lessig argues, because there is a constituent power of the people even greater than in the Articles of Confederation or the Constitution, and it is not constrained by either document. If we wish to follow the way the framers went about it, we should just push the Constitution to the side and put in place a new one, ratified, say, by two-thirds of the country.

Besides, we should be faithful to the Constitution as a work of the Enlightenment, just as Madison and Hamilton regarded it. What is the Enlightenment? Immanuel Kant gave the famous answer: it is the emergence from a self-incurred childhood. The framers would be ashamed of the childish way we treat them as all-knowing, or the way we try to divine how they would govern in a world they could not possibly have known. We owe it to them to stop being children who worry what their great-great-great grandparents might think. Personally, I don't care what they would think. They're dead. We have an obligation to the living.

It even seems that the Constitution itself requires the Constitution to change—or that the Constitution as amended over the years has brought us to the point where we should dispense with the Senate. The Constitution of 1787 began as a form of dual sovereignty, in part for the national government, in part for the state governments. Just as there was dual sovereignty, the people had two types of citizenship—they were citizens of the nation and citizens of the states. The important point here is that the House represented the people in their capacity as national citizens, and the Senate represented the state *legislatures* as institutions, indirectly representing the people in their capacity as state citizens. The Constitution, however, is not static but dynamic. It was designed to form a *more* perfect union, and its inner dynamic or logic was to continue perfecting that union and increase our capacity to act as national citizens. It's because of this continuing work—the perfecting of our sense of national citizenship—that we have outgrown the constraints placed on it by state citizenship.

Aside from changing us as we became used to our federal citizenship, the Constitution itself underwent a change, and the Civil War Amendments—the Thirteenth, Fourteenth, Fifteenth, and Seventeenth—rewrote the original intent. The rejection of one person, one vote is in conflict with these amendments. It is often said that the Civil War amendments represented a second founding, subordinating the states to the national government or making clear that our identity as national citizens was preeminent over our identity as state citizens. That's the argument, for example, in Eric Foner's recent book, *The Second Founding: How the Civil War and Reconstruction Remade the Constitution* (2019). The Fourteenth Amendment declares not just our right as national citizens to equal protection of the laws; that is, these broad rights we had as national citizens against the states. The same amendment also speaks of our privileges and immunities as federal citizens. Foner argues, justly, that the Fourteenth Amendment still has not taken full effect. It puts just about everything the states may do under the possible purview of the federal government. It is a kind of legal occupation of all the states by the national government after the war, just as there was a military occupation of the Confederacy. It is tragic that the Congress did not go on to change the representation of the Senate too. After all, anyone can see, contra Lincoln, that not just slavery but the way the Senate protected it had forced upon the country a civil war. But sometimes, in the fog of war, even the victors can make a mistake, just as the Allies did with the Treaty of Versailles.

During the Gilded Age, we had a Senate even worse than the one that led to the Civil War. In that era, the Senate was for sale because the state legislatures that elected it were on sale, and they were too weak to fend off, much less regulate, the new plutocracy. The railroads, the oil giants, J. P. Morgan, and others just bought up the state legislatures or directly bought off the senators. The dark money of that time was bright as day. It was plainly impossible to let state governments go on electing senators, so eventually, the Progressives stopped it. That was in effect the end of the Grand Compromise of 1787 and the idea that the Senate directly represented the states— that is, the states as corporate bodies—and the idea that senators were delegates from these governments. Thanks to the Seventeenth Amendment, we the people, in our capacity as national citizens, now do the electing of the Senate, but if we are acting in our capacity as national citizens, then we cannot pretend the Senate is representing us in our capacity as state citizens. And if it's not representing us in our capacity as state citizens, it is not possibly representing us in our capacity as national citizens.

This is not just an intellectual argument. It's also real life. We can talk about dual sovereignty, or state citizenship, and for some people, they have a real identity as state citizens. But this is 2021, not 1787. To the extent people say, I'm a state citizen, they're pretending. All of us know—even they know— it's not true.

So while the Seventeenth Amendment may have saved the Senate, in a backhanded way it destroyed its legitimacy.

There is an eccentric, far-right set of Americans who keep calling for the repeal of the Seventeenth Amendment—and as preposterous as that is, these people are not wrong to think the Senate makes no sense unless the Seventeenth Amendment is repealed. At any rate, the Seventeenth Amendment arguably saved the country, or liberal government—it came just in time to make possible the New Deal. Yes, there was still the racist bloc like Carter Glass and Harry Byrd of Virginia—after all, they came from states where fewer than 4 percent of eligible Black citizens could vote. And true enough, they did shut down much of the New Deal. But thanks to direct election in other states, there were more senators like George Norris of Nebraska and Robert Wagner of New York. Even in the South, there were racists who were otherwise on the left: Hugo Black of Alabama, for example, or even the horrific Theodore Bilbo of Mississippi, who is featured in *Fear Itself*. In one respect, by cleaning up some of the old Senate corruption, the Seventeenth Amendment worked too well. It gave us a certain number of liberal heroes, especially in the 1960s—senators like William Fulbright or Wayne Morse or Phillip Hart. In my early teenage years, I was smitten by John F. Kennedy's *Profiles in Courage,* a book about senators who took heroic stands, and it was Kennedy who, for me, gave the Senate a kind of existential cool.

Between 1964 and 1966, Lyndon Johnson was able to do his will in the Senate with a freakishly enormous Democratic majority. The Senate passed the Civil Rights Act of 1964, a start to the end of the racial slavery that the Senate had been set up to protect. At that time, it was hard to see the Senate as a problem, as Lincoln and others did just before the Civil War, or as the Progressives did. Filibusters were extremely rare, and under Johnson, that Senate also passed the Voting Rights Act, Medicare, and the Immigration and Naturalization Act. Under that Senate, we were the land of the free. By the time of Watergate and Sam Ervin and the Church Committee, many young people my age had a huge crush on the Senate. I still have my list of heroes, like Sherrod Brown and Elizabeth Warren. Meanwhile, in the US House, for years it seemed to many of us that there were 435 little ants running over to vote when someone rang a bell. Until Adam Schiff and Jamie Raskin, it was hard to pick any one other than the Speaker who had true national recognition. It wasn't until my late twenties, when I worked at the US Department of Energy under Jimmy Carter, that I grasped that the Senate exists to paralyze the country, and I began to appreciate the US House as the branch that, even more than the presidency, represents the people (or it would, if we could ever stop it from being gerrymandered, as I hope the present Congress can do).

But as labor unions collapsed, and as race and Vietnam broke up the Democratic Party, this "good" Senate went back to its bad old ways. Though in part, that was an accident. Some of the best senators had an idea for a rule to limit the racial filibusters, but they accidentally set off their routine use for almost everything. In 1976, prompted in part by Vice President Rockefeller, the Senate adopted a new rule for cloture; that is, for a cut off of debate. In its current form, it permits a kind of pretend filibuster, a "procedural" filibuster, by filing a motion with the chair, which does not require Jimmy Stewart to stand there until he plops but requires sixty votes to get to a simple majority vote. That's right: it takes sixty senators for fifty senators to pass a bill. The reform was that it used to take sixty-seven, but in the old days, the racial filibuster was just used for protecting Jim Crow laws and vigilante lynching, and sixty votes would get rid of these shocking spectacles much faster. But few could see that the "procedural" filibuster would go on to become routine, and filibusters went from being blue moon events to being used over a hundred times a session. In effect, in 1976, we threw away the "good" Senate. In 1993 and 1994, Robert Dole as minority leader used the filibuster to shut down the Clinton administration—or at least the non-NAFTA part that represented the Bill and Hillary of the Left—which then in turn discredited both of the Clintons with the Left and split the party. But Dole's use of the filibuster also destroyed Dole's GOP, which lost its role as a responsible opposition to the party of Gingrich and, later, Trump. Now the GOP could go to even greater extremes ideologically and still have a hammer to stop a more moderate Democratic Party. The bipartisan "good" Senate was gone. Nor is the "good" Senate ever going to return. Yes, it's true, a few in the GOP did vote to convict Trump—the second time, when he incited a mob that was out to kill them. But it's too late. Even eliminating the filibuster is not enough. It could even make the Senate worse. At least the "silent" filibuster was silent. While it is weaker in terms of blocking a bill, a "talking" filibuster can do plenty of damage to the country too. Think of the poison that will spew out if senators like Ron Johnson get to talk for weeks. There is only so much to say in favor of the Proud Boys.

Eliminating the filibuster will not be the end of the supermajority rule that should worry us most. It will not end the two-thirds requirement for approval of a treaty—for an international agreement on climate or artificial intelligence or the other global threats that threaten us as a species. It is bizarre to think that North Dakota or Idaho is going to make the call. The rest of the world will not permit it. Like it or not, unless we fix the Congress, that rest of the world will force us at some point to dispense with it altogether. Rural white America may be fine with environmental Armageddon, but in one way or another, the rest of the world is going to ensure they don't get the final vote.

In the meantime, even if the Democrats have just fifty votes in the Senate, with none to spare, there is at least a window of opportunity to make significant changes in our form of government. First, in the case of the Senate, we have to abolish the filibuster, of course, but then we must offer the District of Columbia and Puerto Rico, and possibly other overseas territories, the opportunity to become states. Neither of these two projects will be easy, and Puerto Rico may not wish to join. But at least in the case of both DC and Puerto Rico, with the long history of racial discrimination that has barred them from admission, there is a constitutional obligation for the invitation to be made.

As to the filibuster, even if the rule itself is gone, it will always be capable of coming back. The only way to kill it for good is by a stake-straight-through-its-heart law enacted by the House and Senate against any supermajority voting rule not specifically authorized in Article I.

Second, we have to invoke the power of Congress under Article I, section 4 (the Elections Clause) to displace any state from using voter or election data to create districts for the US House. I hope we at least lift the filibuster rule enough to pass the For the People Act.

Third, the Congress has to get rid of the Electoral College, or any other device that might again give the White House to the runner-up. The Electoral College is in the Constitution sure enough, but the Constitution does not prohibit Congress from regulating it. Congress passes laws aplenty that regulate the affairs of the executive branch—and presidential elections—without anything in Article I suggesting it may do so. Besides, there is text elsewhere that arguably gives it that power. The Fourteenth Amendment, for example, makes reference in paragraph 2 to the right of the *people* to elect the electors of the Electoral College—by implication, including the state legislatures. And paragraph 5 gives Congress the power to protect that right. Since Congress has that full or plenary power—as we lawyers say—it also has the power to make it a meaningful right to vote. That is, it has the power to ensure that the people, in their capacity as federal citizens, will have a president of their own choosing, without interference by the states. To effectuate that right, Congress could require the states to assign its electors not to one presidential nominee but to all of them based on their respective percentage of the popular vote. This would eliminate any one state from being a battleground state or a situation where the presidency can be held captive to the decisions that just three or four of the fifty states make. It would ensure that all the people in all the states have the same privileges and immunities as federal citizens, the same right to a meaningful vote in presidential elections.

Fourth, it is the moment to pass a bill limiting service on the Supreme Court to no more than fifteen years. There would still be lifetime *judicial* appointments: a justice on the Supreme Court could continue to serve in a federal appellate court or a district court, if anyone dared, after the expiration of a Supreme Court term. Ex-Justice Souter and ex-Justice O'Connor did not lose their judicial appointments when they resigned from the Court. And the bill should provide that in addition to the Constitution's requirement of submitting the nomination to the Senate, it should go to the House as well, because it is the only body that—until we fix the Electoral College—directly represents the people as a whole. It is still the only place, if it were not so gerrymandered, for representing we the people as we really are.

Even if we had majority rule, though, we might not like what we see. That is the biggest question of all. If we had a representative form of government, what kind of people would we be?

CHAPTER SEVEN:

WE NEED EVERYONE TO RUN FOR OFFICE

A ll right, suppose we have majority rule as well as all the reforms that are in the For the People Act. Suppose we even abolish the Senate. Even if we have the right structures, we need to pour the right spirit into those structures.

Isn't it a matter of just electing the right people?

Yes—but who are the right people? The right or best people may be the wrong people. One day, when I was twenty-three and a staff writer at the *New Republic*, my uncle asked me if I would like to have lunch in the Senate dining room with a friend of his who was a senator. Now this was early in 1972, and they asked me as a young person who I might like to see as president.

Harold Hughes, I said. He was my hero. A former truck driver, he had also been an alcoholic who'd gone into recovery and went on to become US senator from Iowa. The senator at our table called out across the room: "Harold! Here's a young man who thinks you should be president. Come on over!" Hughes walked across the room and sat down. I wanted to die! Then Hughes said, "If I'm to be president, I just want everyone in the country to know one thing—if they come running into the Oval Office to say we're under attack, here's the order I'm giving: *We're not firing back.*"

Or so I remember. But it was no surprise that he left the Senate to go into the ministry. I was heartbroken, even if he was right to do so. It was a point that had been made long ago by Max Weber in "Politics as a Vocation": those who are committed to the ethics of the Sermon on the Mount should stay out of professional politics. Hughes himself knew that even if I did not.

It's impossible, by definition, to have the best people in politics.

I have doubts about myself for even trying to do it. It takes a lot of gall to represent anyone at all, even if it is done modestly or without ego. When I ran, I used to have nightmares that I would end up sending big glossy photos of myself into people's mailboxes—without my glasses—and under big capital letters: STANDING UP FOR YOU!

That's when it would be better if you just sat down or got out of politics entirely. It takes a lot more to really stand up for you than just STANDING UP FOR YOU. It is also getting harder to stand up. The digital age has changed representative democracy; by email or tweet, or by screaming on social media, vigilante groups can track down our representatives and cling to them, fury-like, until they vote that group's way. I can well imagine the fear—that panting sense of being chased, digitally—that made so many GOP senators vote to acquit Trump, even the second time, when their own lives were at stake. John Cullerton, my former neighbor, who just retired as president of the Illinois state senate, told the *Chicago Tribune* about the change: "It's the difference from a representative democracy to a direct democracy. . . . So the old model (for voters) is, 'I'm busy, I'm hiring you. Go down to Springfield. Listen to testimony. Make your informed decision. Every two years, I'll check in on you.' . . . And now you just go directly to the legislator (who says), 'We don't need to listen to testimony.

I've got 500 emails and 5,000 tweets re-tweeted saying I've got to vote for this bill.'"

But are we better off in this virtual republic where we give a weighted vote to people in the grip of aural hallucinations? Maybe in the future, STANDING UP FOR YOU will involve hiding from you—or at least hiding from the vigilantes.

The old divide between Edmund Burke and Thomas Paine—over how a legislator should represent the people— seems especially out of date. Here is how Burke, in the eighteenth century, described his view of representation: "Your representative owes you, not his industry only, but his judgment; and he betrays, instead of serving you, if he sacrifices it to your opinion." But Tom Paine's view, while much better, is troubling too. When there are so many more people for a legislator to represent in our day, and some are screaming, while others are not paying attention or even voting or even aware of who is in office, it is delusional to think, like Paine, that you are transmitting the will of the people. You start sending out brochures: STANDING UP FOR YOU!

I'm damned if I know the right way to do it, but here's what, if elected, I might have tried. I would have tried to do it the way I try to be a union-side labor lawyer. When I was younger, it would bother me: "Why is the lawyer making all the decisions?" Well, the lawyers do end up making too many decisions in effect. But I think the lawyer, as much as possible, should be giving the client the capacity to decide without the lawyer—or at least the lawyer should work to get out of the client's way. Everything I do should be in the service of pulling them into the work of making their own choices and governing themselves.

In the same way, it seems to me, the most legitimate way of representing people is to give them the capacity to do the work of governing or to find some way to pull them into doing the work of governing.

That's not quite direct democracy. Rather, it's the obligation of giving as many people as possible the capacity to replace me in office or giving as many people as possible the ability to be a candidate for office. That is the spirit we should pour into our institutions, and it's the best way to bind people to the UNION in Whitman's sense, or at least to keep that UNION from cracking up.

It would be something different from just more public employment. We have enough public employees, at least at the state and local level. Rather, we should figure out how to let more of us perform an "office" or be accountable to someone. It is to let people have an opportunity to carry out the work of government. That's what the New Deal did with such success. Franklin Roosevelt gave people *something to do*. The New Deal's genius wasn't in the Social Security check, the first one of which did not arrive until 1940, but in the way it allowed just about anyone to walk in, without any fuss, and be part of the state or perform some office related to the New Deal. That's what recovered a capacity for self-government and a level of maturity or political judgment just in time for World War II. It's what helps to explain, in other words, why Philip Roth's *The Plot Against America* is just a work of fiction.

Of course, it helped in the 1930s that there was a state of emergency, but ordinary people could just sign up for the work of the Civilian Conservation Corps, or the bridge building and art making of the Works Progress Administration. They could take part in cooperatives or people-based initiatives like rural electrification or soil conservation—especially in the rural areas, where there is now nothing to do, no exchanging of gifts with those of us in the global cities. The New Dealers pulled people into dozens of projects and classes, not just in FDR's New York but in Alf Landon's Kansas, which led to a sense of being part of the state.

But the biggest way that people felt part of the state was the New Deal project of getting everyone into a union. Unlike labor law today, people in the 1930s in the big plants and mills of the Midwest could just walk in and sign up. In the coal fields, John L. Lewis had his organizers handing out flyers: "The President wants you to join the United Mine Workers." While labor unions belong to civil society, not the state, the early New Deal mass unionism had some of the character of a state project. Yet in the chaos of that period, anyone could sign up. Any outsider could be a union member or a shop steward or a strike leader, if not an officer. It was a way of multiplying the offices for which people could run. There are still ways we can use new forms of representation within corporations—not necessarily union office positions—for which people could run. One example is co-determined corporate boards, which require a business to offer seats on the board of directors that are elected by employees, not stockholders, and for which any employee can run. As to other ways of being part of the New Deal, the work of government now is professionalized, and there are boundaries to keep out amateurs and volunteers. By the time of the Clinton and Obama administrations, the capacity of the state had shrunk, because unlike the New Deal, there was nothing for ordinary citizens to do.

Indeed, the offices of citizenship that existed during the New Deal have disappeared. Sure, there are still juries, though at least in federal courts, judges have fewer jury civil trials, or any civil trials at all. Yet as late as the early 1970s, when I was in law school, jury trials were still common. Once in a while, juries could still not just apply the law, but also decide what the law itself should be. This was improper by then—it was called jury nullification. Yet on occasion, juries once wielded that power. In the last resort, the people still could rule.

Of course FDR's government—unlike the Clinton and Carter administrations—had the advantage of being a response to a catastrophe. It was an even greater catastrophe than the Biden administration now has to face. Just as catastrophe can bring out the worst in people—and bring Hitler or Mussolini to power—so can it bring out the best in a country with a democratic culture, as it did in the case of the New Deal. Consider the argument made by Rebecca Solnit in *A Paradise Built in Hell: The Extraordinary Communities That Arise in Disaster* (2010). Keynesian economics can now head off a catastrophe like the 1930s. It did so under Obama. Though it is with misgiving that one should say so, it may have been better for Obama had there been no such thing as Keynesian economics. Its existence deprived Obama of the moral luck that FDR had. Better knowledge removed the need to sign people up to do the work of government. Of course, Obama's failure to take on the filibuster also allowed an opportunity to be lost. Yet it took that failure for the Democratic Party to give up as it has on bipartisanship, and perhaps—I hope—to dump the filibuster. Biden, who would not seem likely to take on the filibuster or overthrow bipartisanship, has had the moral luck of coming in after Obama, the failure of bipartisanship, and the greater twin catastrophes of the pandemic and Trump. It was also a piece of moral luck to have the Proud Boys and Oath

Keepers rampage through the Capitol: it has at least created the conditions for "extraordinary communities" to arise if the administration is able to give them something to do.

The pandemic, of course, has created an "extraordinary community," at least of those who wore masks and looked out for each other. Still, it has not been as great as it might have been. Besides, we have an enormous, if not bloated, health care sector that does not require us to volunteer in the way we would have had to do fifty to a hundred years ago. Still, for the next pandemic, we should start now to put a civic volunteer infrastructure in place; let people feel already that they are doing the work of government. But there are two other crises that ought to be calling these "extraordinary communities" into existence.

First, the planet is on fire. And not just on fire, but beset by drought, hurricanes, tornados, and floods, a disaster that Keynesian economics or monetary or fiscal policy is partly unable and partly too late to stop. This time it really will be *The Worst Hard Time,* to take the title of Timothy Egan's 2010 book about the Dust Bowl in the 1930s. We will need "community," or an expansion of self-government, on a scale that would dwarf even what took place in the 1930s. It is true that democracies are inherently unable to do the forward thinking to head off global warming—but they may be better at mobilizing these "extraordinary communities" when Armageddon comes. Part of a response to global burning ought to be citizen action at the local level, if only in the form of fire watches or block-by-block Red Crosses. We should already be thinking of new governing structures, staffed with volunteers, that will help carry out environmental goals. If nothing else, we may need such extraordinary communities to help parts of the population relocate to higher and dryer land. We should be thinking now as to how to prepare people on a volunteer basis to carry out the work of the state, if not right now, then by 2030 or 2040. If the ownership of private property becomes an office in a time of global warming, we will need local volunteers, not just government bodies, to see that the duties of such an office are performed.

Second, as COVID-19 has now forced us to see, our country is getting old on a scale that will require even our bloated healthcare system to bring in volunteers. In the decades ahead, with increasing longevity and falling birth rates, there will just be too few of the "young," or those under sixty-five, to take care of those over eighty-five and ninety. Nor is it prudent or desirable to devote too much of the economy to caregiving. We should not keep pulling people out of the workforce to do this kind of thing. In northern Europe, there are already spontaneous "civic enterprises"—not state sponsored, not set up by foundations—where some of the "young," in their spare time, and older, retired, but physically capable citizens visit and watch over the old and infirm. While that used to be the work of the churches, in a post-Christian Europe, it is becoming the secular work of citizens who are volunteering for the state without the state being in charge.

Such communities can save us from destructive forms of individualism. In the Reagan Era, Robert Bellah and the coauthors of *Habits of the Heart* (1985) warned what might happen if the bonds of Biblical and civic religion that once checked that individualism would continue to erode. Well, they snapped—at least for a part of the population. That's how we got to Trump. At a certain tipping point, too much individualism can turn people into a crowd. When there is no community to protect us, it is only in a crowd that we feel safe. I think it's that sense of safety that many people had when they rallied for Trump—the paradoxical sense, as Elias Canetti wrote in *Crowds and Power,* that it's only in a mob that we feel invulnerable and even incapable of being touched. It may be at a Trump rally that some felt they were safest from the pandemic.

It may be a fitting, Dante-like punishment for our hyperindividualism that we have had to live in such isolation from each other. It is another piece of good timing for Biden to be coming into office now—another piece of moral luck. After being locked up for so long, so many of us will be ready to spring into each other's arms.

It would be awful to lose the moment, to fail to give people some work on behalf of the state to do. Fortunately, in another piece of moral luck, there is one very big thing we can do. And it's to that big thing I'd now like to turn.

CHAPTER EIGHT:

MAKE LABOR THE FOUNDATION OF DEMOCRACY

April 5, 2021. Right now, as of this date, the big cause of my imaginary House term is the particular labor law reform passed by the House this year. So far "Protecting the Right to Organize"—or the "PRO Act"—has garnered scant notice. But in this bill, organized labor went big—bigger than in its 2009 bill, known as the Employee Free Choice Act, or EFCA, which went nowhere under Obama.

This old-fashioned cause would do more than single-payer healthcare or a Green New Deal to transform the country. Had we a labor movement, we'd have already had single-payer healthcare. We'd be on to the Green New Deal. We'd not have lost the white working class to Trump. Forget thinking up more strategies on globalization or neoliberalism: it's not as complicated as we make it. We just need a labor movement. I already mentioned Kathleen Thelen. In her 2014 study of European social democracies, *Varieties of Liberalization and the New Politics of Social Solidarity*, she showed that in many of these countries, social democracy did just fine, despite globalization and some deregulation. Rather, in each country that she studied, it was the degree of solidarity that determined how well social democracy survived, be it the size of the welfare state or the state's relative income inequality.

And in each country that she studied, it was the strength of the labor movement that determined the degree of solidarity. It's the strength of the labor movement—and in each country, who is in the labor movement and who is not—that makes Germany like Germany, or Denmark like Denmark. Yet it's the operating notion of some on the left in the US that we can leap into a European-type welfare state with labor's share at just 6 percent of the private sector and dropping. For the Left in the US, the Sanders Left, or even for some old neoliberals who want to be cool, the labor movement is still in second or third place. It's an obligatory mention, far behind single-payer healthcare, the Green New Deal, or a guaranteed income as a cause. Their premise assumes we can get to a European-type welfare state without a European-type labor movement. We can have solidarity without a structure of solidarity. We can get to Denmark without Denmark-type wage-setting institutions.

So would the PRO Act get the labor movement past that 6 percent? As far as I can tell, few people on the left, unless they work for unions, know what is in it. For one thing, PRO would bring back the secondary boycotts that the Taft-Hartley Act banned. It's odd to think that the repeal of Taft-Hartley—what turned people out to elect Harry Truman in 1948—has so disappeared as a cause. How many now know what a secondary boycott is? The PRO Act would also bar employers from "permanently" replacing those who strike. Just these changes alone might let loose again the mass organizing we had in the 1930s.

But are we strong enough to go back to the 1930s? We the people are now a more frightened people, and individualism is an even bigger part of the culture—we may be incapable of solidarity. To help bolster our nerve, the House bill makes organizing even safer. If people want a union, they don't have to have that first strike to get a contract. At least for the first time, a tripartite panel will dictate the terms. In effect, the government will do it: set the wages, everything. See? The idea is, once is enough. Then the parties will learn to live together.

There is a double approach in PRO. As in France, it will be easier to strike and rush the barricades, but as in Germany, it will be much more likely we can sit down and work it out together. Still, it's chilling to think that a GOP administration could set wages. At least doing so might call the party's Trump-Era bluff that it's really on the side of the working class. Still, the bill depends a lot on a friendly National Labor Relations Board (NLRB).

For me as a union lawyer, the best part of PRO is that it lets workers sue directly for violations of their rights. All right, I admit, for me personally, it's good for business. It's also a big stick, something made to order for a much more individualistic country that's much more used to individual civil rights suits than the enforcement of collectivist-type labor laws that unions control. Like Title VII of the Civil Rights Act, this is a private civil remedy, with rights to legal fees and injunctive relief, and—even more importantly—all the powers of civil discovery of documents and depositions. The only limit on the right is that the NLRB has failed to act. It's a change that came from the late Congressman John Lewis, hero of the civil rights movement. And it opens up labor law for everyone to enforce—not just unions with limited legal budgets.

It also opens up new ways for workers to emerge as leaders. Inevitably, by being union officers, they will end up on the left, even if they started out for Trump. That's the great prospect—it won't just redistribute income, but it will also redistribute power, as the New Deal did. It has the potential to create leaders not just *for* but *from* the people who voted for Trump—leaders who may not even have college degrees.

It's no wonder that the Retail Federation of America called the PRO Act "the worst bill in Congress." I even wonder if I should call attention to the bill's existence. Maybe it's better that I say nothing. But then it may not happen if the Left in general says nothing. The danger is that those who should be for it may be relatively indifferent to its existence.

Yet in any pundit's piece on Biden's program, who mentions that bill or sees it as transformational? Likewise, on the left, everyone has to make an obligatory mention in favor of it. "Of course I'm for it!" Of course—and that's the end of that. It's single-payer healthcare or the Green New Deal that inspires all the passion. Some may even suspect a cause for which Biden is all in, even if he keeps saying, "I am a union guy."

Besides, is it enough to be transformational? *That's* what the Left should ask. Talk to any organizer: people are out of the habit of joining labor unions. A single working mom who should be in a union decides she can't be involved. She has enough going on in her life. So I am sorry to say, as big as it is, the House bill is not big enough. Maybe it's big enough to keep the labor movement from disappearing or dropping below 6 percent of the private sector workforce. Maybe it's enough to get to 12 percent, though it's doubtful. Even that's just a doubling. We need a tripling. We need 18 percent or more. We need the point where labor is strong enough to keep the Dow from rising and can siphon off some of what's there now into people's paychecks. Then we will start to close in on European-type solidarity.

To get there, one more thing is necessary. The federal government has to force all its private contractors to have unions, as it did during World War II. That includes every contractor and vendor who lines up for Biden's proposed $2 trillion for an overhaul of the nation's infrastructure. That may sound shocking. It's not evenhanded. But a nation-state like ours has three good reasons for forcing this type of unionization. First, a revival of a labor movement—even if forced—would be a form of political and moral reconstruction. It would be a way of detoxifying the culture. It can reintroduce Trump voters to the norms of democratic citizenship.

It is necessary for a labor movement to be an instrument of macroeconomic policy. It creates a wage-setting institution. It's a way of managing the economy, as presidents as late as Nixon used to do. It would be especially urgent now as a way of increasing aggregate demand by getting people out of debt.

Last, but far from least, a revival of labor is a necessary if not sufficient condition for ending racism. For racism will not end until there is an end to the country's extreme economic inequality. Otherwise, without a labor movement, people are just marching to change the boards of theater companies or to get meaningless high fives from universities and banks. Nothing will change. Martin Luther King Jr. knew it. He was murdered leading a strike.

We will have to mandate a labor movement, mandate employers or at least federal contractors to have collective bargaining agreements. We are moving into a time—and a world—in which the labor market has never been weaker. Even if we could get the PRO Act intact, it is hard to revive a labor movement with unemployment over 10 percent. That's a world no one in organized labor under the age of sixty has ever known. Over the next five years—or maybe ten—we will find out what the world is like.

How do we force federal contractors to have labor contracts? Congress has to change the Procurement Act. Let's put that condition on the $2 trillion-dollar infrastructure plan, to whatever level that money goes. To have a federal contract, or to be the recipient for federal assistance, a collective bargaining agreement should be in place. There is a precedent, or close to one: during World War II, the Roosevelt administration forbade workers from striking but pushed employers to recognize unions. It was a wartime economy. Washington, DC, was everybody's customer. It also did the rationing and the controlling of prices. Employers had to ask for permission to raise prices. Controllers like the young John Kenneth Galbraith could ask: Where's that collective bargaining agreement? In this pandemic, or the next one, or in a future of global warming, the federal government may be the biggest customer in the economy again. When Biden calls for infrastructure spending, he says it is going to create *union* jobs, and at least on the radio, he comes down hard on the word *UNION*. Well, if the law changed, it would be in his power to command it. There have been only two waves of union organizing in the country. The second big wave—as big as the first wave in the 1930s—took place in this country during World War II, in the early 1940s, by informal decree. The Left prefers to celebrate the first wave, but it's the second that is just as responsible for why there is anything left of labor today.

The old reason to mandate unions, as Galbraith set out in books like *The New Industrial State*, was to create a "countervailing power to business." It is still a great reason.

Even before the pandemic, the big firms were getting bigger. The story is set out by Thomas Philippon in *The Great Reversal: How America Gave Up on Free Markets* (2019). With the pandemic destroying so many small businesses, the big firms now will be even bigger—and better at busting unions.

More than ever, this statement in section 1 of the Wagner Act applies:

> The inequality of bargaining power between employees who do not possess full freedom of association or actual liberty of contract, and employers who are organized in the corporate or other forms of ownership association . . . tends to aggravate recurrent business depressions, by depressing wage rates and the purchasing power of wage earners in industry and by preventing the stabilization of competitive wage rates and working conditions within and between industries.

Yes: that was the law of the land. Those are the words of the statute now. You may notice that it is a statement concerning how to run the economy. The right to join a union was an instrument of macroeconomic policy. It was a form of Keynesianism, or stimulating aggregate demand, before Keynes wrote the book on what Keynesianism should be.

Now, in this time of the burning of the planet, it is a form of environmental policy too. We have to move people double time out of fossil fuels and into green jobs. There is legitimate pushback or worry that green jobs will not pay as well. Let's remember, though: fossil fuel jobs, in coal and steel and other sectors, did not pay either until the New Deal made them pay.

Very few hourly jobs pay until we make them pay. Right now, with a pitiful 6 percent of the private sector workforce, organized labor is hard-pressed to raise the wages of its own members. But should it become 36 percent, it could raise the wages of its own members and everyone else's. That's why it was once—and could be again—a way of managing the economy.

Even without that motivation, raising wages serves a great Keynesian cause—getting people out of debt and boosting aggregate demand. As at least some economists have written, that's what fiscal and monetary policy are less and less able to do. In various ways, they can sap the purchasing power of workers. The purpose of monetary policy is to make it easier to go into debt. It has the effect of increasing inequality by transferring income from the debtor to the creditor class. Even fiscal policy is a way of going into debt and increasing the transfer of income from the federal budget to creditors. Labor law reform all by itself is a way of stimulating demand without running up a debt.

It is also a way for a political reconstruction—a point I made in the last chapter. It would give people a chance to learn to govern themselves again. That's the way the British and US occupation authorities used the labor movement in Germany after World War II. It is remarkable how closely they worked with many young trade union officers who were just out of the Wehrmacht or set free as POWs. It was a way of detoxifying the culture. In a similar way, we on the left have to counter Trump's power with the working class. Of course a big increase in union membership will not mean that every new such member is sure to reject Trump. But it will increase the number of those who end up holding a union office, be it local recording secretary, shop steward, or even just sergeant at arms. At least *they* will be aligned, almost by definition, against the GOP. The younger they are, the more likely it will be true. It's a way of reintroducing people to civic norms by giving them a new right to vote for officers of their own choosing.

Finally, it is a way for racial reconstruction with a hard dollar value. In 2019, a study from the Center for American Progress compared, by race, the median wealth of union-member and non-member households. For Blacks, the difference is as follows: $22,106 for Black union households, and just $2,371 for Black non-union households. For Hispanics the difference is also great: $33,696 for union households, and just $3,093 for non-union households.

That's a tenfold increase in wealth on hand for every Black person who joins a union—an increase of 486.1 percent to be exact. Yes, white union households have even higher wealth. That's in part the accident of being in the last redoubts of a fossil fuel economy. Otherwise, an expanded labor movement might be of greater benefit to Blacks than whites, as Blacks even now are slightly more likely than whites to join unions.

But there is another reason why a big gain in union membership—for all workers—is the best way to racial equity. Under a union-free form of capitalism, with huge disparities in income, someone will always end up as an untouchable; someone will have to be at the bottom of the pile. Perhaps I have missed it, but there must be some professor who has argued that as the form of capitalism changes, so will the form that racism takes. What is racism now is both the same and much different from the racism that Martin Luther King Jr. fought against. Racism has changed as the country has gone from a relatively social democratic form of capitalism, which could have been made truly open to all Black people, to a liberal meritocratic capitalism, which is never going to be. As well argued by Branko Milanović in *Capitalism, Alone,* and by others, too, this meritocratic capitalism is rigged, not just in terms of financial capital, but human capital as well. It has had the effect of raising some Black Americans to dizzying heights, even to the White House and dream jobs at Harvard, while nonwhite working people are looking up at this elite from further down than ever before.

This is not the capitalism that King or Bayard Rustin knew when they marched on Washington and pushed for what became the Civil Rights Act of 1964. Their strategy was premised on there being a New Deal, and it might well have worked had a labor movement which Blacks could join stayed intact. It might have worked had the New Deal not gone away. Well, it did. Suppose we were able to flip a switch and end racism as we know it. Even a color-blind version of inequality would still leave millions of Black Americans in poverty, and even more living paycheck to paycheck, so long as union membership stays at the rate it is now.

It is hard to believe we can keep our inequality in place and just rid it of its racism. Suppose big checks in the form of reparations for Black Americans were handed out. How long, under our form of capitalism, before that money would be gone? The necessary precondition for reparations would be to put in place a new form of capitalism in which they are not going to be stolen. Like the white working class, the Black working class can save, not individually, but collectively. They do it through collective bargaining—and by putting money into funds that they do not control.

For many Black Americans, it may seem too much to ask—emotionally—to accept that the best way to raise the wages of Black working people is to raise the wages of white working people as well. But the only way to go forward is to let everyone onto the Brooklyn Ferry and start to go across. It is often said that right now we need "a national conversation on race." It's even the slogan of big corporations. Of course we need such a conversation, but we have been having such a conversation ever since the 1950s. Maybe, as marriage counselors tell unhappy married couples, we should try doing something together instead of talking our problems through. Like the working people I represent as a labor lawyer in unions, more people of all races should be in these unions and just *doing* something together.

Maybe they will be doing it only out of self-interest. But it is at least sometimes true of unions what Alexis de Tocqueville once wrote of New England town meetings. It may be, Tocqueville argued, that the participants first get involved out of self-interest, but the meetings end up transforming people when they work for shared goals.

In such a way, we might get from labor unions to UNIONISM, which Whitman was trying to describe. Or it is one of the ways we can try again to enlist the hearts of the people in keeping the UNION in place. Many years ago, my old college teacher, and later friend, the great Samuel Beer, sent me an essay he wrote on Whitman, which was never published in a book. I have it here on my desk:

"Tom / as promised: my model of the national community."

For Whitman, Beer wrote, the democracy that would enlist the hearts of the people would come out of the division of labor, all those occupations that Whitman is so good at noticing. From all of these would come a common purpose, uniting the "grand races of mechanics, working people and commonality." For Whitman, we must become aware how all of us are conferring gifts on each other, and how these exchanges—in the workplace, or within the family, or on the farm—are not just heroic in themselves, but the bonds of our political union. UNION or UNIONISM depends on conferring the greatest possible dignity on these exchanges.

Dear Sam, it is my model of a national community too. That's why I keep this essay on my desk. It's there to remind me of the gifts we confer upon each other, just as Whitman saw it, for it may be the only way we will learn to govern ourselves again.

EPILOGUE:

WE'RE ONLY FREE IN PHILADELPHIA

Though everyone discouraged me, I originally meant to end this book with a quote from Whitman—the opening lines from "Song of Myself":

I celebrate myself, and sing myself,
And what I assume you shall assume,
For every atom belonging to me as good belongs to you.

See what he's saying? *"I'm more like you than you are."* He's just being a real American—he's running for office.

But I decided there is a better way to end all this brooding about representation, and it's to describe a suit we brought in Philadelphia, the home of the Constitution, to challenge the gerrymandering of the US House districts in the state.

For years, in a half-hearted way, I had tried to peddle the idea of challenging gerrymanders of the US House under the Elections Clause, or Article I, section 4. The legal challenges up till then had been under the Equal Protection Clause of the First Amendment. But the germ of the idea was in Justice Anthony Kennedy's concurring opinion in *US Term Limits v. Thornton*, which held that state laws requiring term limits for members of Congress were unconstitutional. The court, with Kennedy concurring, held that a state legislature had no power to impose term limits because a state legislature could not get in the way between the people and the national legislature.

So if that was true, gerrymandering of the US House was even more illegal—it was the state legislature picking the party representation of the people sent to Congress.

Yet no one had ever brought this type of challenge. For years, my friend Alice Ballard and I had talked about this legal theory. "It's so logical," she said. Instead of saying that a state legislature could not gerrymander "too much," so as to violate equal protection, our claim under the Elections Clause was that there could be no gerrymandering at all.

And the worst gerrymandered state of all—worse even than the GOP gerrymander of North Carolina—was the GOP gerrymander of Pennsylvania. And Alice was in Philadelphia. Why not . . .?

No, it was too hard. It would be too expensive. We had no one behind us. And I would have to stay at a Marriott and I couldn't afford it.

So I tried with Common Cause, and they said no. Then I tried the ACLU, and they said no. Then Public Citizen said no, too.

Wait: why not do it on my own? I had wasted $300,000 in running for Congress. Well, that money was gone, and there was no way to pay it back. But maybe by filing this suit I would be working off that debt as a kind of community service.

Rather than be in the House, I could fix the House—or be a part of trying to make it the House of Our Dreams.

And, of course, a case like this was way too big to try. But I told myself there was no way we were ever going to try it. But I thought it would be something just to get the case on file. It was 2017, Trump was in, the GOP had the House, and our side was out. But Justice Kennedy was still up there, and the court at the time had a major gerrymandering case it was about to decide. So maybe if we filed, one of his law clerks would take note of our legal theory, and in our small way, we would contribute to a five to four decision against gerrymandering with Kennedy in the majority at least in part because of what he had said previously about the Elections Clause.

That's all I thought that Alice and I could do. The Supreme Court would decide, and it would be over, and we would never be going to trial.

So we filed on October 4, 2017, no doubt too late to affect the 2018 election. Fine, we were just lobbing it out there. We put out a press release, got on local public radio, and to my astonishment, even got a call from the *New York Times*. The question: "If this is such a good claim, why hasn't Common Cause or the League of Women Voters brought it?"

"I . . . well . . ." (I couldn't say I had begged them.)

I made a note: Next time, no press release to the *New York Times*.

But now came a much bigger shock. The judge, Judge Baylson, wanted the parties before him next week—that is, just seven days after we had filed. Usually, it would be months. Then, in the status, he set the trial—I mean a full-blown evidentiary trial—for December 4, 2017, literally within two months after we had filed. I don't mean a preliminary injunction but the whole thing—before a three-judge court, with experts and graphs, a warp-speed expedition of what normally would take five years of discovery.

It would take a whole book to describe how we dropped everything in our lives—just like in a House election—and scrambled to do more than thirty depositions in the next two months. Brian, a lawyer friend of Alice's, bumped into us at the status hearing. Could he help? My God, yes!

I was terrified the Friday night before the trial. I had to figure out the opening. Out at O'Hare, to distract myself while waiting for the plane, I bought a copy of *Devil in the Grove* (2011), set in the 1940s, about a Florida murder case handled by Thurgood Marshall. The book won a Pulitzer, and as I tore through it Saturday night in my hotel room, how I wished I could have been even close to the kind of lawyer that Marshall was: to hang out in the nightclubs of Harlem when Harlem was cool, to drink and smoke and party and then hop a train from Grand Central and go South, way down South, to the barbaric pit of a rigged US legal system, and yet somehow get acquittals for Black men who had been set up or framed, or, if he didn't win at trial, figure out how to keep them from being lynched while setting up these heartbreaking appeals, which often went up to the US Supreme Court, until he knew every justice and, in some cases, could break into a justice's poker game to get him to scribble his name on a stay, and then heading back down to the South, and often being hunted down at risk of being lynched himself because he was winning too many cases, and all while polishing the arguments for the biggest case of all, a challenge to official racial segregation of the public schools, pushing inexorably on to *Brown v. Board of Education,* which in 1954 turned out to be the beginning of the end of Jim Crow.

As I lay in my hotel that night and kept reading, I was more affected than in my first week of law school, when on a Friday night I saw Jimmy Stewart in *Anatomy of a Murder* and decided I should keep going on to be a lawyer. That's how I felt all over again: *I wanted to be a lawyer.* So what would I say to anyone considering law school?

It's this: stay away from *Devil in the Grove.*

Besides, if I really wanted to be that kind of lawyer, I'd have been in Alice's office that night helping her prepare the exhibits.

The trial went great, the discovery had been gold. Their witnesses blew themselves up on the stand. So what happened?

We lost two to one. Or really one to one to one, since no two judges agreed. The worst was the Obama appointee, who had been hostile from the start. That's no surprise: it's a pretty carcerist bunch.

But with the two Republican appointees we had a chance—a good chance, even though we were challenging a GOP gerrymander. So I thought I would end this book with the closing argument I made, or at least one part of it, as I like to remember it:

"May it please the Court," I began, "there are two ways to think about the case you've heard—two different perspectives that come from two different Supreme Court justices. The first is that of Justice Kennedy, whose opinions on the Elections Clause we have cited. It's his view that nothing—nothing—should get between the people and their representatives in the national legislature. The states have no business getting in the way. That's what we have argued—this is a case to restore the Constitution's design, to get the states out of the way of picking winners and losers.

"But there's still another way to think about the case before you—it's the perspective of Justice Souter, who just retired. And he was asked in an interview at that time what worried him the most. And I'm not quoting exactly, but this is close—he said, 'It's not a nuclear war, or attack by an enemy that is the greatest danger to the country now. The greatest danger is that *the people do not know whom to hold accountable.*' This court—this court—has a chance to be accountable to the people, to give them back the right to choose their own members of Congress. Yes, this court could be . . ."

Here I have to stop. I can't remember the whole thing. But I know the chief judge gave me a look as if to say he understood, and for a moment, from that look, I thought, "Oh my God, we have a chance to win."

But in the end we couldn't get him. He agreed that there had been gerrymandering but held it was a political question; that is, it was not up to a court to decide. It was the kind of thing for which a court could not be held accountable.

And Justice Kennedy resigned a little later, so he could not be held accountable.

But the third judge, Judge Baylson, also a Republican appointee, decided he would be accountable. He wrote a 119-page opinion setting out a better argument than we could hope for as to why the plaintiffs were right on the facts and the law, including the claim under the Elections Clause.

And there is a kind of happy ending; though we lost, a similar state case brought by the League of Women Voters started the following Monday in state court and put in much of our evidence and argument. And the state case did win—the state Supreme Court was full of Democrats—and there was a new map in time for the 2018 election, which led to more Democrats being elected and helped the Democrats take back the House.

Some people thought it was our case: "You saved the country." It's painful to keep saying, no, actually, someone else saved the country.

Though Sean and Mike and Alice and Brian should get the credit for this amazing work, here's the one thing I take a personal pride in: not once did I say, in this case tried in Philadelphia, that the Constitution was drafted just two blocks away. Or maybe it's three; it's past the Dunkin' Donuts. No, I didn't say it once because I figured that in federal court in Philadelphia, they hear that line all the time.

Yet it was just a few blocks away. And I used to think, that week in Philadelphia, we are free to change the way we are governed. And there are people in this country—yes, some of them Republicans—who are ready to be held accountable. We're only free when we're all in Philadelphia and learning as a people how to govern ourselves again.

But it's true, to quote Whitman, the word "Democracy" still sleeps. The History of Democracy has yet to be written.

ACKNOWLEDGEMENTS

I apologize to everyone on whom I inflicted a draft of this public policy novella. Special thanks, or perhaps apologies, to Jim McNeil, Shanti Fry, and Elliott Gorn, who reread drafts and had valuable suggestions. Thanks also to other readers including Theresa Amato, Nicolo Majnoni, Lew Sargentich, Tony Judge, Rick Bank, Stephen Holmes, Leonard Rubenstein, George Sheanshang, Helen Hershkoff, Dan Lewis, Sidney Blumenthal, Tom Donnelly, Tim Noah, Joel Brenner, Ed James, and others I'm forgetting. A thank you to Lawrence Joseph for telling me where the title of this book was. I had good advice also from the late Marshall Sahlins. I owe much to Chris Lehmann, Jason Linkins, Emily Carroll, Sarah Fan, and Lee Froehlich for their edits of various freelance pieces that I spun off while writing this book.

Thanks to Mike Persoon for holding together the firm when at odd moments I would disappear to write or rewrite.

Above all, I am grateful to Belt Publishing—to the publisher Anne Trubek and my wonderful editor Martha Bayne. The two of them made the book so much better. Thanks also to Michelle Blankenship for her help in launching it into the world.

And this note to Chris Lackner—as usual, you came through for me again.

I also thank all of you and the other millions who voted to dump Trump a few months ago. But for you I probably would have lost the heart to finish the book.